ABOVE GROUND

RESILIENCE TO OVERCOME. STRENGTH TO SERVE BOLDLY.

BY

ALLAN FRANCIS

ABOVE GROUND

RESILIENCE TO OVERCOME, STRENGTH TO SERVE BOLDLY

Hardcover ISBN: 978-1-961098-81-7
Paperback ISBN: 978-1-961098-80-0
eBook ISBN: 978-1-961098-82-4
Printed in the USA.

Joan of Arc Publishing
Meridian, ID 83646
www.joapublishing.com

TABLE OF CONTENTS

Table of Contents

DEDICATION

To my One and All—my beloved grandmother, mother, father, and my life-saver, Mervis McKenzie Davis. Every part of my being is a reflection of you. Your love, kindness, and selfless servanthood have shaped me in ways words can scarcely express. Your sacrifices, compassion, and guidance laid the foundation of who I am today. This book stands as a testament to the unwavering support and love you have given me and to the man I strive every day to be. I carry with me the legacy you built with such care and devotion, and that's why my love for you knows no bounds. Though my heart aches in your absence, I celebrate you and all that you represent, wishing you were here to share in this moment.

With endless love

Allan

ABOVE GROUND

ACKNOWLEDGMENTS

I am profoundly and forever grateful to my amazing family and friends who walked alongside me on this intense journey of bringing to life "Above Ground."

To my beautiful wife Wendy Francis - Thank you for your unwavering support, love, patience and encouragement. We did it! Thank you for trusting and believing in me. I love you always. To my four incredible children who I could not possibly disappoint, Allan Jr, Rain, Corey and Denzel - thank you so much for your critical input. I love you all to the heavens. To my brother Eric Morgan - thank you. We are two of a kind, and I love and appreciate you so much brother. To you both Colette DeAcklen and Kimberly Francis, just know how important you are in my life and our children's lives. Those bounds will never be broken. You have my love and appreciation always. To Gabriele Hill-Gomez and her loving family, special thanks to you Gabi. Our friendship seems like a lifetime, with so many beautiful memories. Thanks for taking such great care of me while stationed in Germany, love and appreciate you. To Rebecca Ray, friends come and go, but you stayed. I treasure the wonderful years of knowing you, the memories and the laughs, the spontaneous activities that we were always ready for. I love and appreciate you very much. To Linda Michelle Denney, how can I thank you enough? You have done so much for me, you pushed me and guided me to the critical resources needed for my book to come to life. I will never forget your kindness, love, and especially our friendship, my amazing BFF. I love you always. To my best friend and brother Brandon Jones and his lovely wife Maryori Jones, my sister, you both mean so much to me. I hold you both in high regard, and I love you both like no other. To the United States Army and my Military family, you adopted me when I had none, I found my first family in you. Thank you for the opportunity to grow and to become the leader I am today. I am bound to you in love and service to our great country, the United States of America, forever. To my publisher, mentor and friend Keira Brinton and her entire Joan of Arc (JOA) Publishing team—thank you for believing and seeing the vision I had for "Above Ground" and for bringing it to life with thoughtfulness, care, skill, expertise and passion. To my editor, Seth Czerepak, you embodied my vision from day one, you saw through my eyes the impact I wanted and you delivered without missing a beat. Your expertise and commitment are deeply appreciated, thank you so much. This book is a reflection of all of you, and I am honored to share this journey with such an incredible circle of friends and supporters.

UNLOCK YOUR EXCLUSIVE BOOK BONUSES!

Thank you for reading *Above Ground*! I've prepared a collection of exclusive resources just for you.

HOW TO ACCESS YOUR BOOK BONUSES

Simply scan the QR code below with your phone to unlock your exclusive resources:

A HEARTFELT LETTER
TO MY READERS

For Moms and Dads,

Moms and Dads, this book is a gift to you. What if my mom had read this book? Would she have still left me in Jamaica, left me with strangers? I don't think so. And Dads, if my father had read this book, would he have still abandoned me? Maybe not.

This book is essential for every mom, dad, grandmother, godmother—every person with a human heart. This book is not just for you; it's also here to help you become a better parent. By reading my story, there are many things you might no longer take for granted. Maybe you'll pay more attention to your child. Maybe you'll be more available to your children. Maybe you'll think twice before having children, and if you do, you'll be more present to ensure you don't make the same mistakes my parents made.

This book is a valuable resource for you, your daughter, your son, and anyone in your family as they have children of their own. Think of this book as a family legacy to pass down through the generations. You may have a cousin, uncle, or aunt who will benefit from reading this book. Anyone who reads this book can find themselves stuck in a hole. My story shows the way out.

I got out. Read my story, and you will see how faith, trust, hard work, and never giving up can lift you to the very top. When your hands bleed, you pull harder; when your feet hurt, you push further; you walk faster. You have to reach for life above ground, for that is where you stay alive and live your best possible life. Let nothing deter you from that; let nothing stop you from living your best life.

This book is for every one of us.

For Teachers and School Officials,

Teachers and school officials, have you ever wondered why your classroom sometimes feels like it's in disarray? This book, *Above Ground*, is for you. You need to understand the demographic of your classroom—all students were created equally, but not all have had equal opportunities. *Above Ground* will help you understand those who come from less privileged backgrounds; it's important for you to know and recognize them.

You might notice certain behaviors in your classroom and wonder why a particular student is acting out, displaying erratic behavior, showing attitude, appearing depressed or sad, crying at times, or sitting quietly by themselves. These could be signs of early depression, and as a teacher, it is perfectly normal—and essential—

for you to intervene and ask questions like, "How are you doing?" or "How was your day?"

You'll learn a lot about these situations from my story. It will help you look at kids or someone in your class with a different perspective, perhaps seeing what lies beneath their surface behavior—feelings or experiences that I discuss in my book. People who see me in real life would never guess, even for a second, the kind of life I've lived. When people hear my story for the first time, it often seems unbelievable or even ridiculous because of my achievements along the way.

Of course, I never allowed myself to be cheated out of my life or my dreams, but that's my story—Alan Francis. Not everyone has that same capacity, strength, or faith. So, it's important that communication is maintained in the classroom. It's crucial to observe behaviors, to talk, and to connect with your students, making sure you do your best to reach every single one of them.

This book is for you, and it is also for your students. It will help them understand that even someone like me, who struggled and faced enormous challenges, was able to overcome problems—whether they were related to life's difficulties, abuse, or personal pain. Your students may face different challenges, and understandably, they may have different concerns or behaviors. Prejudices exist in the world, but finding common ground is essential.

My story will help you better reach students who display certain behaviors or face unique problems. Perhaps it's not that they don't like math or English—maybe there's a deeper issue at play. My story will give you some new thoughts and strategies for understanding and connecting with them.

For My Military Family and Comrades,

My deepest regards and love to those of you in my military family, those in and out of uniform, my comrades in arms, families, and friends of the military. You were and will always be my first real family. Without you, I'd be only a shadow of a man. I would have lost myself in my abandonment, my sadness, and my loneliness.

Every military personnel values this one thing above all: being and staying "Above Ground." That's where we take our stand; that is where we engage those who would dare to trample on our freedom, our liberties!

Some of you, I'm sure, have walked in my shoes. I've met many of you along the way. So, I extend to you this book, my story, our story *Above Ground*, with my most heartfelt gratitude and admiration for the military, my family. It's my most valued, my most precious possession—my legacy! I hope you will see me as I see you!

As a 22-year Army combat veteran, I know from a very personal standpoint what we deal with day in, day out—the cross we bear, the sacrifices we make, the ultimate sacrifice some are called upon to pay. I hope you will find some refuge, some comfort, trust, faith, beliefs, and healing words within these pages.

My memories, my pain, my struggles—all of them kept me moving. They enhanced and fortified my mindset. They challenged me to reach for the higher calling of putting service above self, taking nothing for granted, and having a thankful heart for each and every blessing bestowed upon me.

To my military family, just know how much I love and appreciate you. I was a lost, broken young man, and you took me in your warmth, mentored me, and helped me to become the warrior, the soldier I am today. No more feelings of loneliness—enriched, sincere, and endless family members and friends to call upon. May God continue to bless and keep our family safe!

To All Humans... I See You

This is your journey, but you will never have to travel or walk alone. I have been exactly where you have been. I've walked in your shoes in my most difficult times. I've cried many tears. I've hungered and thirsted for the basic necessity of love, from a mom, from a dad. I was abused in the most tender years of my childhood—scars yet to be dissolved.

I see you, clear as day—as I see myself. *Above Ground* is my gift to you. It will be your companion in hardships; it will be your place to find refuge; it will be your place of peace, love, and contentment.

Above Ground will take you on a new journey—one of life and living, no longer a victim, but a conqueror. You will see my smile on every page regardless of my past battered predicaments, the evils I had to withstand, my sadness, the blurred lines—yet my zest for life: to fight, to trust God, to walk in faith, blinders on, to live happily and courageously—not by default, but by my own design.

You are either in two places in life: "Above Ground" or "Below Ground." Obviously, below ground we will all be one day. Not for you nor I today, because above ground is where we are called to overcome, to live, to experience life with all its complexities and happy ventures, to make memories way beyond what we have ever dreamed, ever imagined! To love, to smile, to give, to share, to support, to grow, to build, to be your totally amazing self.

I implore you to not just read this book, this gift, but to LIVE IT WITH ME!

PART I

MY JOURNEY
ABOVE GROUND

CHAPTER 1

MY MOST
PAINFUL MEMORY

There's a certain stillness that comes with the Jamaican heat, where the sun hangs like a burning ball in the sky, and everything beneath it feels both alive and exhausted. The bushes around my little house rustled in the wind. I was just a child then—barefoot and curious—living among the wild things. As a kid, I was mischievous, always curious and full of questions, eager to learn, and sometimes stubborn, like most kids are.

It was on this day that I was close to the bushes alongside the house, cooking out of a tin can. I was heating up dumplings on a little makeshift fire that I had made just for this moment. While I was sitting there, carefree and happy, the fire caught on to some nearby bushes. I quickly was able to put it out before it got too far. But before I did, my Godmother saw what was going on. She rebuked me, slapped me around, and gave me the harsh notice: "Wait until your Godfather gets home."

My Godfather was the most feared person in my life then. He was ruthless and unforgiving. When I think of him, I think of the word wicked. As the day went by, my heart was beating like a thousand drums. I was in so much pain and agony with just the thought of the whipping, the beating, the abuse that was yet to come. I remember crying profusely, wiping my tears away a hundred times, but my tears never stopped raining down my face.

Then the dreaded moment arrived when he finally made it home, and he began calling my name with a belt in his hand. I was scared. I had spent hours fearing this beating, so I started running toward the bushes with my bare feet.

I rarely wore shoes, not by choice, I learned to live without things I don't have, so barefoot was my normal attire. I ran as fast as I could, but he was right behind me. The terror racing through my body distracted me from the path ahead. There, on the path in front of me, was a dreaded cactus patch. These were cacti that fell from the cactus trees, and there was no way of running around them. The bushes were thick, the cactus covered the earth, and I could not run back the other way. I would've run directly into my Godfather's belt and horrific beating. This was not an option. I could not stand another beating today; my body was too frail from the other beatings.

SADLY, I WASN'T FAST ENOUGH

As I ran through and across the cactus bed barefoot, I felt no pain— my fear of the beating had rendered my body numb. But he caught up with me at the very end of the cactus path, which was about 20–25 meters long. Suddenly, my feet, once invincible to pain, could no longer hold out; the agony came crashing down on me like a tidal wave. Blood gushed from my feet, and it felt like a million thorns were being driven into their soles. At that point, the beating would've been less painful—I welcomed it; I surrendered. It was over, I thought—just beat me to death. But no, I wasn't that lucky. He said to me:

"The way you came is the way you are going back."

Sure, I was okay with that, not knowing what he actually meant.

My 8-year-old brain assumed he would pick me up and take me over the cactus path—after all, my feet were bloodied and already dead. But then again, why did I expect such mercy, such compassion? One step at a time, he dragged me back through the cactus path, each step bringing another million thorns of pain.

We made it over the path. Then he dragged me up to the house and beat me. We were like two boxers in a ring, with one being bound while the other did all the punching. Finally, it was over; my body limped, and I could not feel my feet. At that time, the first aid for such injuries was to dip my feet in kerosene oil, which my Godmother willingly provided—oh, such motherly love.

I couldn't walk for two weeks. Healing was a slow process, but slowly and painfully, I overcame the injuries from the cactus path and the wrath of my Godfather, and I was able to walk again.

I often wondered: would this be my life's condemnation—pain, misery, beatings, hunger, and hopelessness? What about love, something I haven't discovered yet, never known, never felt? Something I craved with each battered breath. Is love not for me too? Am I not part of the human race?

THROUGH ALL THIS, I WONDERED...

Mama, where are you? Can't you see these abusers have no love for me? Mama, are you coming back for me? Deep down, my soul is slowly dying—Mama, please come back for me! Jamaica, London, England—that's your choice to be, but you gave birth to me, then you left me with strangers who have no love for me.

My innocence, my youth, caught up in a state of child abuse. Mama, where are you? I know it's not normal to go to sleep at night with hunger as my only appetite. I know it's not normal to walk the streets while the blazing sun burns my bare feet. So many lonely days and nights have passed, and I have never once heard your voice.

I'm stuck in this hole—is this my destiny? Little did I know that this question was about to define my life and my mission.

CHAPTER 2

OUR JOURNEY STARTS HERE...

At some point, you may find yourself in a hole. A hole so deep, you'll fear that it's your destiny to stay there. Maybe your hole is a dead-end job, a bad relationship. Maybe it's a sickness or a sudden betrayal by someone you love. But every hole has a top, and that means there's a way out. There's a way back above ground.

I have been at the bottom of a pit, a hole, one that had no ladder, no exit sign, no easy escape push button. No yelling or calling out would ease my terror or speed up my escape. I have borne the brunt of hunger to the point where I chose to fall asleep earlier, as a child—at 7 PM versus my normal 10 PM—just to avoid feeling the pain of hunger, to not hear my stomach turn angrily like the waves crashing on the shores after a terrifying storm. I know the terror of physical abuse and wanting to die at eight years old to escape the pain, the suffering of it all.

I am sharing my stories to help you see what is possible. Some of my stories might be hard to read, but please read them and use them to help you get out of YOUR hole. You may be at the bottom of that hole right now, staring up at the walls, wishing, praying you could find your way out—or facing somewhat similar conditions to my very own terrifying experiences.

If I was able to climb out of mine, I know without a shadow of a doubt you will be able to do the same. Let Above Ground be your guide. Let's journey together—your fight is mine; we win and overcome together.

This book is my journey out of the hole. I was able to go from being an orphan who was rarely fed more than bread and sugar water to eating at some of the finest restaurants on the planet. I will share with you my story, my embarrassments, my disappointments, my troubled heart, my terror—not for self-pity, but to help all who may be so inclined to join me and walk in faith on this journey. To lift each other up, to share love, compassion, and understanding, to bond together and break free from the evil that has bound us.

LIFE IS TRULY A BLESSED GIFT

Once you're above ground, there are no limits to your greatness. There is nothing you can't do. There are no demons you can't conquer. You can choose to live a life designed by you, instead of by default.

I believe that life is a gift and that if you are above ground, then you must live it as such. I want to invite you to trust me because I know what it's like to fear that the way back out will be as painful as the way you came. But if that horrid day in the cactus patch taught me anything, it's that the way back is never the same, because YOU are not the same.

You're a stronger and braver person than the one who fell (or climbed) into this hole. And the moment you find your way above ground, you'll discover exactly who this new person is.

CHAPTER 3

THE STRANGER WHO
SAVED MY LIFE

My early life was full of pain, suffering, and hunger. I never knew my mother. She left me after my birth.

Not only did she abandon me—she left me with strangers. Horrific humans who delighted in the torture and abuse of a little boy. They were called my God-parents, but there was no God within them. They were dark, and my life was one of lack and abuse.

If you understand the suffering that I endured, you'll understand what I chose to do at eight years old. I decided that I was going to end my life. There was no way out of this hole I had been thrown into. No doors, no windows, no ladder. Death was my only exit strategy.

OR SO I THOUGHT...

I remember that day as if it were yesterday. I had a plan. My plan seemed as quick and painless as possible. I walked to the nearest gas station where big truckers came through regularly. I watched as a driver went into the gas station. Then, I ran down to his truck. I quietly snuck near the tires and slid myself under the truck, right in front of the tire. And then I waited silently for the truck to move and end my life of suffering.

As I lay underneath the truck, the driver finished fueling his vehicle and climbed into the driver's seat. When I heard the engine start, I knew the truck was about to leave. I felt a sudden relief knowing that I would never have to take another beating or feel the brutality of immense hunger.

The minutes felt long as I lay there, waiting for it to finally be over.

Suddenly, I felt this huge pain in my rear. I thought it was the pain of dying. Instead, it was the driver. He had come back around the truck a second time, saw me lying there, kicked me, and cursed at me to run off!

I thank God for him today and for the jolt of pain he caused me. If it weren't for that man coming around his truck for a second time, I would not be here today.

I know he was inspired to get out of his truck, walk around it, and find me. I know now that God wanted me alive. It was not my time to be below ground. God knew what was ahead for me. He knew that the life I would eventually live would be greater than that eight-year-old could ever imagine. I am alive today because God moved through that stranger driving the truck. I believe this happened not just for me, but for everyone reading this book.

I AM HERE TO WRITE YOU THIS BOOK...

I often wonder how an innocent eight-year-old, so desperate and hopeless that he was willing to end his life, could become the person I am today. Today, I am a leader who gives hope to others, shares with others, loves others, and encourages others. If you met me today, you would never guess the suffering I endured as a young child. I have not let the physical scars take my joy. I do not live in bitterness or resentment toward those who hurt me. Today, I find gratitude in everything. I have become the strong military leader that I am because of the strength given to me to survive those early years.

Maybe you have felt this before—the feeling that being below ground was better than continuing in your current life. You may have planned your own exit from this world. Even if the exit wasn't suicide, maybe you just wanted to get away—to go anywhere.

I understand.

But let me tell you…

If you're in a hole now, you don't know the life God has for you. I can also tell you that your past does not define your future. You can be whatever you want to be. You just have to get up, stand up, and decide to live life to your fullest potential.

THIS IS MY WISH FOR YOU...

I wish to see you rise up, no matter where you are, and discover the life God has in store for you. I was in the deep. I was in the darkest places of my life when I started this journey. I had no hope. I thought my life was over before I even knew what living was.

And here I am now. Here WE are. I'm happy, loving, sharing, and saving lives. I could not be more appreciative of my journey, even my painful past. More than that, I'm happy to be sharing this journey with you. So, don't mistake this part of your journey as a bad thing. It's only bad when you're in the middle of it. The good comes when you realize who you've become because of it.

I understand how bad it feels when you're going through it. I lived it, I breathed it, and I suffered through it.

But let me tell you something magical…

Today, I use my journey as fuel for my fire and zest for life! That's why I am so passionate about being Above Ground. Today, this means more than just being physically alive. It means having another day to live, to fight, and to learn—on our terms!

How can you put your current situation into a bigger and more hopeful context?

CHAPTER 4

STARVING - FIND FOOD - EAT FOOD - LIVE

I have spoken a lot about the physical abuse I endured during my first ten years of life. I wish that was the extent of it. But it wasn't.

I lived in hunger every day of my life.

I remember being seven years old, trying to fall asleep early just to avoid feeling the deep hunger pains raging through my body. But I still had to wake up, feeling worse than before. If we were lucky, we got one slice of bread and some sugar water. The severe lack of food made even this meager portion enough to fill my empty stomach. The hunger made me so weak it was hard to move. And then, I had to withstand the harsh beatings from my Godfather. This was far too much for the small frame of a young boy's body.

BUT HERE'S WHY I NEVER COMPLAINED

Since I was deprived of food, I ate whatever I could find with gratitude—even food I picked up off the street. I felt deep gratitude for any meal put in front of me.

There was only one day a week when my stomach would be filled to capacity: Sunday afternoon, after the movie ended at the drive-in theater. My best friend and I would get low to the ground and crawl along the side wall, careful not to be spotted as we trespassed. This became our weekly Sunday ritual—the best meal of the week.

We learned that patrons would dump their leftover food boxes outside their cars, while those sitting in the bleachers left theirs by their feet. As soon as everyone abandoned the theater, we were in position, ready to scavenge.

When the hunt began, we climbed over and under the seats in search of the best food. We looked for the heaviest boxes because they contained the most.

We showed up at the movie theater hungry, but we left full. The constant nag of hunger was finally gone. Afterward, we would lay there in deep contentment and satisfaction. Grateful to have found food. Grateful not to be hungry.

Sometimes we left with our arms full of leftovers, enough to last another day or two. These moments taught me an important lesson about gratitude.

When you have nothing but a slice of bread and a cup of sugar water for dinner—or sometimes no dinner at all—you learn to appreciate what others throw away. These Sunday feasts kept our hungry bodies going. The movie theater provided better meals, but garbage cans were also a valuable source. We picked out the best we could find, as long as it wasn't spoiled or foul-smelling.

This was my reality for quite a while. Starvation was no longer a condition. We had found multiple sources of food. God was good— we weren't hungry anymore!

HOW I FOUND GRATITUDE IN SUFFERING

I am grateful for my years of painful hunger. They taught me to live a fully grateful life. Each time I eat now, I feel deep gratitude for every bite I take.

Hunger also trained me to find solutions to other problems. The skills I acquired during those years of searching for food helped me lead more effectively in the army. I saw problems and found solutions faster than my peers. While I would never wish the pain of hunger on anyone, I know I was meant to endure it. It made me the man I am today.

I didn't make my meals; they were provided for me—not in the traditional sense, and not as traditional meals served at a table. I give God thanks every day for those meals. My only concern was to rid myself of hunger and stay alive. Those years taught me that you can't be both a beggar and a chooser. You must understand your battlefield and your predicament and navigate accordingly.

Survival is the key: eat, and you'll be able to fight and live another day.

When I was hungry, I didn't get to cook my meals or choose what to eat. I worked with what was in front of me so I could live one more day to create the future I wanted.

THIS APPLIES TO MORE THAN JUST PHYSICAL HUNGER

Have you felt the pains of hunger in your life? Maybe you've never been physically starving, but you may have experienced a deprivation of love, connection, or peace. Maybe you've felt starved for friendship, happiness, kind words, or someone to believe in you.

Maybe you feel this pain in your body—aching and throbbing—reminding you of what you want but don't have.

When this pain comes, remember my story.

When I was starving, I didn't succumb to hunger. I found solutions and filled my belly with what I could. I did this knowing that, if I lived another day, I could fight for something better. Don't give in to your current deprivation. Find gratitude in what you have so you can create what you want and fulfill the desires of your heart.

Hunger is inevitable, but starvation is a choice. You don't have to give in to hunger or let it steal your hope.

FIND GRATITUDE AND KEEP FIGHTING

No matter what you're hungry for right now—whether it's love, peace, or joy—don't give up. Gratitude for what you have now will fuel your journey to what you desire. Use your hunger as motivation to fight for a better tomorrow.

And always remember: you can survive, thrive, and rise above.

CHAPTER 5

ONE BREATH AWAY
FROM DEATH

Young kids often follow others and do foolish things. I was no exception. One hot, sunny day, when the air shimmered and the ocean glistened under the relentless sun, I found myself with a group of friends at the beach. I was just eight years old and not much of a swimmer. I could tread water a bit, but that was the extent of my abilities. My friends, much older and braver than me, decided it would be a great idea to venture out into the deep water on an old truck tube.

They kept insisting that I join them. I resisted, a knot of fear tightening in my stomach, but one of the boys grabbed me by force, dragging me to the tube. Before I knew it, I was clinging to the thick, black rubber—the only thing between me and the endless deep water. As they paddled farther from the shore, my fear grew. I held on even tighter to that tube, my lifeline.

The tube was large, likely from a big truck tire. There were five of us in total, all gripping it with both hands. At first, the others seemed content just to float. But soon, boredom set in. The boys began jumping off, splashing around, and acting crazy, as kids often do. I watched them, wide-eyed and terrified, knowing there was no way I would join in. The water was too deep, and I was not a swimmer. My fear gripped me tighter than I gripped the tube.

Then, suddenly, one of the boys jumped off with a big splash, and the tube shifted violently. I felt myself slipping, my hands losing their grip. Before I knew it, I was going down, down, down—plunging deeper into the dark water. I could see the surface above me, but it felt miles away. Panic set in. I thought…

"THIS IS IT—THIS IS HOW I DIE."

As I sank, my arms flailed desperately. I couldn't breathe; my chest tightened, and my lungs burned. My vision blurred with salt water. Then, as if by some miracle, I felt something—a piece of clothing brushing against my hand. Clinging to that thread of hope, I gripped it with every ounce of strength I had left.

It was one of the older boys, a strong swimmer. By sheer miracle, he had been underwater at that moment and felt my frantic tug. Realizing I was in trouble, he pulled me up to the surface. When my head broke through the water, I gasped for air, my lungs flooded with relief and pain. I coughed violently, my body trembling, my eyes burning from the salt.

The others, who had been laughing and playing just moments earlier, suddenly realized the gravity of what had happened. They hadn't even noticed I had slipped off. No one had been looking for me. It was only by God's grace that the boy had been there when I needed him most.

The boy who had initially dragged me onto the tube was the first to speak. His voice was shaky as he suggested, "We should go back in. Now." Everyone nodded in agreement, fear evident on their faces.

It's Not Your Day to Die...

As we paddled back to the shore, every stroke felt like a slow-motion replay of my life. When we finally reached the sand, I stumbled out of the water and collapsed, my body heaving with sobs. My chest burned with every breath, my eyes stung from the salt, and I coughed and vomited from the water I had swallowed. Everything had happened so fast, yet it felt like I had been underwater for hours.

As I sat there, the fear and pain began to subside, and I realized something profound. I knew God Himself had a greater purpose for my life. Death would not claim me that day. It was not my day to die. I had been pulled from the depths, and I knew there was more in store for me.

Looking out over the vast ocean that had almost swallowed me whole, I felt a strange sense of peace. I was alive. I had been given another chance. And with that, I knew—I was meant for something greater.

I learned that day that God knew me and cared for me. God had saved me, and I wasn't about to waste this life He gave me.

When You're in a Hole...

When you're in a hole, God may seem far away. When my godfather was beating me, I wondered where God was. But the truth is, God is always near, even in the darkest of holes. The question is whether we choose to see Him—not with our eyes, but with our faith.

You're Not Alone...

Some of history's greatest heroes found their destiny at the bottom of a hole.

Look at Joseph from the Bible. He was literally thrown into a pit, with the intention that he would die. But God saved him from that hole and later created a life of abundance and joy for him. Joseph was blessed with many gifts that he later shared with the same brothers who left him in the hole for dead. As he shared, God blessed him with riches and abundance.

When Joseph was stuck in that hole, do you think he could have imagined what his life would look like in the years to come? Never.

Look at the story of the Old Testament prophet Jeremiah.

Jeremiah was thrown into a pit filled with mud so deep that the only place to look was up. He was going to die there, swallowed by the sinking mud. But a slave came by each day to feed him a slice of bread, keeping him alive.

When Jeremiah's faith returned, God delivered him through the actions of the king. The king commanded 30 men to retrieve Jeremiah. From that time forward, with Jeremiah's faith reinstated, God made him a leader and protected him from persecution. But Jeremiah didn't find his faith in these blessings. He found it in the hole—and the blessings came after.

The Purpose of the Hole...

When we are in our deepest holes, the only place to look is *up*. That's where we find our purpose. It's where we find ourselves. The hole is never meant to bind you, but to test your faith and your will to survive. Everything that happens makes you stronger. It prepares you for your true purpose. No matter where you are, know that you are being prepared for a much larger mission and a higher calling!

CHAPTER 6

MY ANGEL, MY GRANDMOTHER

Throughout my life struggles, unknowingly, God had already delivered me from the evil that beset me. My safe place had already been provided for and established.

There was a deeply spiritual woman everyone called Aunt Tina. She was like an angel, always bringing Godly messages. Her life was simple, and she carried a huge basket on her head to transport fruits for sale—a custom typical of Jamaicans in those days. Her basket was filled with red sweet plums, mangoes, sugarcane, and other fruits. Every few weeks, she made her rounds, and one of those stops was near where I lived. She would stop to talk to me, offering me plums and mangoes. One day, out of the blue, she shared a secret: she was praying for me and planned to speak to my grandmother, Mervis McKenvie Davis, about me coming to live with her.

The feeling was immense; it was the best news I'd ever received. I immediately began imagining my new home with my grandmother— a woman I didn't even remember meeting. Months passed, but I never lost faith. Deep down, I knew it would happen. I don't know how long it took, but the day finally came when I was invited into my grandmother's home. I started smiling again, and suddenly, life seemed so different. For the first time, I wasn't scared for my life anymore.

My grandmother was a humble woman, poor in material wealth but rich in spirit, love, and humanity. She had the most beautiful heart on the planet. Her big, warm smile sometimes revealed a hint of shyness or modesty. Adjusting to this new life was easy for me. I came from nothing, brought nothing, and appreciated everything—every word from her mouth.

I vividly remember the first time my grandmother told me she loved me. I paused, confused, my young brain scrambling to comprehend. "What does 'I love you' mean?" I asked.

She turned to me with a smile and said, "It means someone cares for you, protects you, takes care of you, feeds you, helps you to be a good person, teaches you respect and manners, and makes sure you are happy and healthy."

I WAS COMPLETELY BLOWN AWAY.

No one had ever said such words to me before. At 11 years old, why was I just learning about love? More importantly, why had I never been loved before? Yet, I realized that long before my parents, the world, or even I understood, God Himself had loved me. He had always been there, guiding me through the toughest moments. I had spoken to Him many times, cried out to Him, and often felt joy and relief afterward. Though I didn't know the word "love" in that context, it was His love that had carried me.

In my new life with my grandmother, I had to learn many new things: self-care, making my bed, saying grace before meals, washing dishes, cleaning the house, and sweeping the yard. My grandmother even taught me how to cook. It was truly a life transformation.

Schooling became another priority. Having been taken out of school abruptly and not returned until my grandmother rescued me from my godparents, I had no concept of kindergarten, first grade, or second grade. At ten or eleven years old, I couldn't read or write. Every evening after public school, my grandmother and uncle became my second set of teachers. They worked hard with me, sometimes using tough love. Before long, I could read and write. Learning excited me, and though I wasn't the smartest, I quickly caught up and even surpassed some students who had been in school their whole lives.

Church was a part of our routine. My grandmother, a Baptist, walked with me about a mile and a half to church every Sunday and sometimes during the week. I became deeply spiritual, realizing there was a Source far greater than my parents—God, whom I could call on for help, just as I did when I felt buried in despair.

The Ladder of Hope

I learned that being "below ground" didn't necessarily mean death. It represented bondage, crushed dreams, lack of opportunity, abuse, and deprivation. My grandmother became my "Ladder of Hope," rescuing me from a life of despair. She was the angel who lifted me from the depths of loneliness, grief, and pain.

This was my second chance—moving from a life near death to a life fully lived. It shaped my attitude and mindset forever: living in gratitude, taking nothing for granted, and appreciating every moment. I had no reason to complain anymore. My life had been returned to me, and I chose to live each day with a thankful heart.

Do you remember your Ladder of Hope? Was it a loved one, a neighbor, a stranger, or perhaps God?

Or maybe you're still waiting for your Ladder of Hope to arrive. Rest assured, it will.

This book might be your Ladder of Hope. Let it give you strength, shield you, and lower itself into your hole. All you need to do is grasp it and start climbing.

A Letter to All Women

To all grandmothers, mothers, and women on this planet, I am so thankful for you. I was never abused by a woman. It was my godfather who abused me—years of unjust whippings, beatings, being pulled out of school, barely having enough to eat, and working like a grown man. All of this ended when my grandmother rescued me at age 11.

As a child, I feared men. Walking down the street, if a man approached, I would cross to the other side. I saw men as abusers, as enemies—that was all I knew. Women, by contrast, were always kind, caring, and protective, just as my grandmother was. I owe a debt of gratitude to each and every one of you. I see you, and I honor you.

Now that I am older and wiser, I understand there are many great men and fathers. I no longer carry those feelings toward men. But my gratitude for the women who have helped and protected me will always remain.

CHAPTER 7

BREAKING CHAINS: THE FIGHT TO LITERACY TO LEADERSHIP

I knew nothing about kindergarten, first grade, second grade, third grade, or anything that resembled a normal school experience. My early years of education were abruptly cut short. I was pulled out of school with no explanation, and I didn't set foot in a classroom again until my grandmother rescued me from my horrible godparents—people I came to see as nothing less than evil.

At age 11, I was starting over from scratch, barely able to read or write. The world of learning was an unfamiliar place to me. It was a space that had been kept from me. Now it had opened up like a new horizon before me.

My grandmother, determined to make up for lost time, didn't waste a moment becoming my first true teacher. Every evening, after my day at the public all-age school, I would come home to another round of schooling—this time with my grandmother and my uncle.

They were tough on me. They had to be. It was their version of tough love, which sometimes involved a whipping here and there to keep me in line. But more often, it involved hours of reading, writing, and going over lessons repeatedly until they stuck. They were relentless because they knew how far behind I was.

It wasn't long before I could read and write. The process of learning awakened something inside me. It felt like discovering a whole new world that had been hidden from me. I took a deep interest in learning. I wasn't the smartest kid on the block, but I found myself passing others who had been in school their whole lives. The thrill of learning new things and catching up, even surpassing my peers, became my motivation. I developed a near-insatiable hunger for knowledge.

From Catching Up to Getting Ahead

By the time I reached high school, I was not just keeping up—I was excelling. I held several leadership positions and became the drill sergeant of our marching band drum and bugle corps. The role came naturally to me, and I realized early on that leadership was a big part of who I was. I loved helping, sharing, and guiding others, and I thrived in positions where I could bring people together, inspire them, and lead them toward a common goal.

An Unexpected Turn....

Years later, my journey took an unexpected turn. I was blessed with the opportunity to travel to the United States of America. It wasn't long after I arrived that I enlisted in the United States Army. I found myself stepping into a new world—a world of discipline, training, and constant challenges. Playing soldier was no game. The field exercises, deployments, day-to-day training, and schooling were exhausting, stressful, and daunting. But for me, it had to be done. I had set my mind on achieving a college degree. I was a perfectionist and fiercely ambitious.

While most of my peers enjoyed their evenings and weekends, I confined myself to the barracks, studying relentlessly. When they were out at parties, I was hitting the books. There was nothing I wanted more than to move up in rank, to be promoted faster than my peers. I knew it would take sacrifice to reach my goals. I had come from absolutely nothing, so missing out on any opportunity was an absolute no-go. Every chance to advance was a lifeline to a better future, and I clung to that with everything I had.

Earning my degree was not a straightforward path. It took several years, as I wasn't attending college on a traditional civilian schedule. But I pushed through. I majored in Computer Information Systems and Business Management through St. Leo University in Florida, attending an on-base campus whenever my schedule allowed. I also earned multiple certifications, including Network Certification, CompTIA Certification, and Network Engineering Certification, among others. These credentials were not just pieces of paper. They were keys to opening doors that had once been shut tight.

Climbing the Ladder...

My advanced education became my ticket to early promotions as a Non-Commissioned Officer. Later in my career, it led to my selection and advancement to the rank of Chief Warrant Officer. Each step up the ladder felt like a victory over the circumstances that had once tried to keep me down.

But my journey didn't end there. I continued to pursue further education, driven by the belief that knowledge is power and the understanding that every new skill learned was another step toward securing a better future. I completed three degrees and countless certifications, each one a testament to my relentless pursuit of excellence.

My story is not just about escaping a difficult past. It is about rising above it. It is about realizing that no matter where you start, no matter how hard the journey, there is always a way forward. It's about never giving up, taking every opportunity presented to you, and having the courage to dream beyond the limitations of your circumstances.

More Than a Survivor

Through it all, I learned that I was more than just a survivor. I was a leader, a learner, a fighter. As I look back now, I see that every step of the journey, every chAllange faced, every hardship endured was preparing me for something greater.

I came from nothing, but I have achieved so much more than I could ever have imagined or dreamed possible. And I know that my story, my life, is just beginning.

You don't have to do everything right the first time. You don't have to get it perfect on the first try, and things don't have to line up right away. I wasn't able to attend school at a young age, but that didn't stop me from becoming the person I am today. It didn't stop me from being promoted through various levels, and it didn't stop me from becoming a Chief Warrant Officer. I acquired the education necessary for advancement, and I made it happen.

What I'm saying is: don't let misfortune hinder you. Even though I was illiterate until I was ten years old, unable to read or write, I still finished high school, went on to college, and not only caught up with my peers but surpassed many of them. This takes being resilient, an overcomer, and knowing that you can change the world.

I have never allowed discouragement to stop me. I may have felt it, but I pushed forward to reach new levels and achieve greater results. Education is important. It has been essential for me because every rank, every promotion above my peers, required a degree. My selection as a Warrant Officer required a degree.

And despite my humble beginnings, my journey didn't stop there. I went on to become the recipient of the Bronze Star and the Legion of Merit—some of the highest decorations in the Army. These honors were given not because I was the most talented or because everything came easily to me, but because I persevered. I earned those awards because I refused to let my circumstances dictate my future.

The truth is, no matter where you start, what really matters is how you choose to move forward. Life will always present challenges, but your story isn't defined by how long it takes to achieve success or where you begin. It's defined by your determination, your perseverance, and your belief in what's possible.

As I reflect on my journey, I realize one thing above all: it's never too late to begin. You are never too far behind. The only failure is in not trying. So, take that first step—however imperfect it may be—and trust that the path will unfold. This is only the beginning. Your story, like mine, is still being written.

CHAPTER 8

THE GHOSTS OF THE PAST

The memories, places, and remnants of military combat never leave me. Today, I sat on the beach, continuing to write my book. The beach was calm—just perfect, not too hot. People were all around me, and birds flew by. As I began writing, several important thoughts came to mind. I managed to jot down a few lines before someone walked by, and I lost my focus. I tried to regain my concentration and continue writing. Then a bird flew in front of me. I glanced up at the seagull, which seemed to look back as if wanting to start a conversation. Again, I lost my focus.

People kept walking in front of me, some sitting nearby, talking amongst themselves. My mind wandered, scanning the crowd—beside me, around me, in front and behind me. In public spaces, I often find myself in a combative mode internally, constantly looking over my shoulder, always vigilant, ready to protect those around me from some unseen enemy. Sudden loud sounds trigger me, putting me into a defensive stance, as though preparing for combat. Someone walking up behind me heightens my awareness even more, shifting me into an offensive posture—ready to retaliate against perceived danger.

This heightened awareness is the gift left to me by the United States Army—a result of combat and a diagnosis of severe Post-Traumatic Stress Disorder (PTSD). My life hasn't been the same since returning from combat. Every night, I dream of it—fighting, evading capture, rescue missions. In some dreams, I've even been shot. I wake up in a cold sweat, praying it's just another nightmare—and it always is.

For a long time, I survived on only four to five hours of sleep each night. Every little noise, whether inside or outside my house, would wake me. To feel safe, I kept several of my registered weapons—guns—right by my bedside. It took me a long time to move out of that mindset, to stop feeling unsafe in my own home.

Putting Your Ghosts to Rest...

It took a while for me to visit my doctor. I was convinced that my behavior was normal for a combat veteran—after all, what do you expect from someone who spent 22 years in the Army? Eventually, I found the courage to make an appointment for a routine check-up. During the consultation, my doctor asked several questions, and that's when I was diagnosed with PTSD—Post-Traumatic Stress Disorder.

At first, I didn't believe it. I thought I was bulletproof, an invincible soldier. I assumed that everything I was experiencing was just the result of my 22 years of military service—always alert and present. But I was wrong. I needed help to deal with what was inside of me, and I received that help. I am so thankful for the United States Army.

I can assure you, help is out there. I sought help, and I got it. I know what it's like to walk down the street constantly watching over your shoulder. I know what it's like to go to a movie theater and search for the perfect seat where you feel safe—making sure no one is behind you. I know what it's like to be in the grocery store, trying to stay composed, but all the while scanning your surroundings. Sudden, loud noises still get to me. I used to instinctively drop to the ground when hearing one, assuming a fighting position, ready to fire. It happened to me two or three times.

I also know what it's like when you start to fear your own friends—not because they've changed, but because you have. I've been there. I've worn those battle scars. But there's help.

PTSD isn't just a result of war—it can come from any kind of trauma, even at a young age. Many people outside of the military suffer from PTSD, so it's not something the Army alone "owns." However, PTSD is prevalent in the military because soldiers are constantly engaging in combat. Soldiers, often young, are thrust into battle, facing enemies head-on. As a frontline supervisor or officer, you might watch a comrade fall beside you. That kind of trauma leaves a lasting mark, a memory of hardship, of loss.

PTSD isn't unique to combat. Childhood abuse or traumatic events later in life can trigger it, too. For example, if you were abused as a child, you might always scan a room for safety whenever you walk into it. I understand this firsthand. When I was young, I was beaten harshly by my godfather. When I walked down the street, if I saw men on one side, I'd quickly cross to the other, avoiding eye contact and hoping not to be seen. At just eight years old, I was already showing signs of PTSD.

The Power in Asking for Help

If you're struggling with PTSD or chronic anxiety, know that you're not alone. As a leader and a soldier, it was hard for me to admit that I had a problem. I had led soldiers into combat, helped them through life-threatening situations, and yet I couldn't admit that I needed help. We're trained to believe we're invincible, even against bullets, even against death. So many soldiers refuse to seek help, which may be one reason we have such a high suicide rate in the military. We're told to be superhuman, to handle it like men—and that's where the danger lies.

But there is help. There are places, agencies, and organizations that provide support for those dealing with PTSD. If you find yourself struggling, set your pride aside. Take off the armor, lower your defenses, and seek the help you need. My life changed after I sought help. While I'm not completely cured—there's still a level of vigilance in me—it's no longer overwhelming. I can control it now. It doesn't own me anymore.

Here's what I've learned: PTSD is not a life sentence. Look at all I've achieved despite my PTSD. If you have it, don't let it be your crutch. Get the help you need, so you can live the life you were meant to live.

Now you know where I came from. You know how I escaped my own hole and got above ground. Let's talk about your journey now.

PART II

GETTING AND STAYING
ABOVE GROUND

CHAPTER 9

I SEE YOU

I have shared with you many of my own stories with utter sincerity and transparency. I did this to show you that I FEEL YOU and I SEE YOU as clear as the sunlight in the sky! Every tear, every pain, every struggle, my heart goes out to you! This is your journey, a responsibility you must undertake, but you don't have to travel alone. I understand your assignment, I understand the cross you must bear. Let's walk together hand in hand, step by step; we are stronger together. I admit, my struggles may be somewhat different from yours, but knowing that there are others out there who have journeyed as you will make the task a little less heavy, give you more clarity, and just like me, you will not be defeated.

This book, *Above Ground*, could not have been written if I had let my past defeat me! Your struggles, your journey, It's not meant to subdue you, to bring you to your knees, but rather, to be victorious at every task, to boldly stand up, to move against the odds, to thrive, to enlighten, to open your eyes and mind, to let the sunlight in, to see the possibilities, to understand the true purpose of your being and that of your creation.

I know what it's like when you're in the depth; that dark deep hole. Zero visibility, blinded vision, the absence of conversations, hearing impaired, hope shattered, the only focus, your entire being begging the question "how do I escape this." Not sure I even knew what faith was at the time. I was too young to comprehend such vast complexities. I needed an angel for sure. Thank God one came.

This was my ladder of mercy. It found me in the depths of my cries, where I felt hopeless and alone. I started climbing to the top, one step at a time, every careful step revealed new challenges. My attitude changed, I became a new source of life, accompanied by the new light I saw above me; the light that speedily enabled my steps upward, on my way above ground, to my freedom!

Service is the Height of Success...

Those selfless acts of service taught me the extraordinary impact of serving others. The effect on me changed my life forever. From teenage to manhood, all I sought was the possibility to serve others. This became the common thread that weaves through my life until this very day. From my humble beginning as a Private in the United States Army, going through the ranks of a non-commissioned officer, selected as a drill sergeant, training over 2,000 civilian men and women, molding them into soldiers—the will and fighting machine of the United States Army.

Eventually, I was selected as a warrant officer and climbed to the rank of Chief Warrant Officer. I served and led men in combat operations. My leadership skills and commitment to my soldiers were evident to my superiors. After 22 years of distinguished and loyal service, I was awarded the Bronze Star Medal and the Legion of Merit. My retirement from the army was short-lived. Within a week, I was bored out of my mind, and so my quest for community service began.

Within a few short years, I was serving as President of the Radcliff Rotary Club, Membership Chair for the entire District 6710, Founding member and President of the Sunset Rotary Club, Assistant District Governor 6710, President Radcliff Chamber of Commerce, President Hardin County NAACP, Legal Redress Chair Hardin County NAACP, Honourable Kentucky Colonel, Appointed by the Governor of Kentucky to serve on the Board of Dentistry; ran for public office as State Representative for the 26th District, President and CEO for my four companies: Bedrock Training Company, Column6 Technologies, Bedrock Cafe, and Bedrock Digital.

I was involved in every facet of my community. I served others with every opportunity that was presented to me. My life after the army was a full-speed marathon; nothing less. I hunger to serve others. I continued this journey of serving others. I trained with the John Maxwell Team as an Independent Certified Life Coach, Teacher, Motivational Speaker, and Trainer. Being a life coach is one of my greatest blessings. I find sheer joy in helping others climb upward, shatter their bondages, and find their way above ground!

Your Ladder of Hope

Part one of this book gives you the tools to live above ground with gratitude, joy, and success. If you're in a hole right now, this might sound impossible. You may be in a place so dark, you can't imagine what light even looks like.

But I can assure you, as the sun will rise, if you walk by faith, gather your strength, make haste with every step, believing that there's a new tomorrow and embrace said belief, you will see miracles unfold.

Imagine when Moses came to the Red Sea, what went on in his head— nowhere to go, cornered in every direction facing the Red Sea. What manner of man would stand firm, believing and trusting his God in such a hopeless place, such a hopeless situation? Who would endure the pressure of defeat, surrender, and accept the slavery?

Not Moses. His faith was stronger than the armies surrounding him, even when the sea was not yet parted.

I was in the same place! That's how I know that, my faithful believer, it's possible. Be a witness to the great works of the Lord, experience the warmth of his love, his compassion, the endless possibility above ground!!

CHAPTER 10

RECOGNIZE YOUR VALUE

If you are stuck and can't see a way upward, this will be the most important chapter in the book for you.

First, know that you are not alone. There are tools and principles that can help you climb out of your hole. These tools have helped other people, and they can help you too. When you feel alone, it's easy to tell yourself that your situation is so unique that no one can give you any answers. This is simply not true.

That's the first belief that will get you out of your hole. The second is to believe that you are far, far too valuable to be stuck where you are. You deserve better.

You might feel like you belong in that hole, as if it's the only place you deserve to be or the safest place you could find. But that's not true. You deserve better, and accepting that is the most important belief of all.

Choose to see your value, even when all outside evidence denies it.

What are you worth? Are you worth just a dollar, or $100, or is your worth infinite? I would tell you that you are priceless. But you need to see that value in yourself. You have to radiate that energy—the energy that says, "I deserve that trophy piece." People should be able to see through your actions and behavior that you are not just a simple human, but someone who commands respect and is worthy of greatness.

I understand that you might still doubt yourself. But trust me, getting above ground starts with one thing: loving yourself. And loving yourself means seeing yourself as a being of infinite value.

When I was a body, I was so desperate to escape this life because I had no concept of love. I had never been loved, so how could I possibly love myself? That's why it seemed so easy to choose to leave. I thought it was the only option.

But I am here to tell you that love is possible. If you feel like you've never been loved and you think it's impossible to love yourself, let me be the one to show you how.

As you grow, you must learn to add value to yourself.

THE GAME-CHANGER: KNOW YOUR VALUE

Remember, the Creator made us in His image. The Creator, with the master plan to design life, would never create anyone who is less than anyone else. You were created as a masterpiece. In God's eyes, you are a masterpiece.

No mistakes.

Let me give you an example. Think about a time when you were able to buy a bike. You've seen pictures of bikes, you've watched others ride them, and finally, you go to the store. You see several bikes on display—some new, some used, and some in need of repairs. You've always wanted a bike.

Now, not all bikes are created equal. If you had the choice, which one would you pick?

Most likely, you would choose a brand new one—the one that makes your heart happy, the one that makes your eyes light up.

In the same way, when God created you, He didn't create an old, worn-out bike. You were crafted as a wonderful, magnificent, extraordinary human being.

That is you.

Owning your value starts with understanding what that truly looks like. Let's use an example.

Imagine you're talking to a close friend, someone you've known for a very long time. There's mutual respect and love between the two of you. How much value would you place on that friendship? If something happened and your friend needed your help, would you be willing to make a sacrifice—even something as significant as losing a finger—to help them? That's one way to measure value.

Now, let's go deeper. Picture this person as your mother, a woman who loves you with all her heart, who has given everything for you. You adore her just as much. What if she needed not one, but two fingers? Would you hesitate? Likely not. You would willingly give up those two fingers because you truly value her for all she's done for you—for giving you life, for loving you unconditionally. You might even give an entire hand if necessary, because for someone like her, the value is immeasurable.

This idea of value can be applied in many ways. You've been through hardships and challenges, and you've overcome them. You know what you bring to the table. You have children who look up to you, who want to follow your example. You are not just an ordinary person—you carry a wealth of experiences and strengths.

Now Ask Yourself This...

How much value do you place on yourself?

Is it the same value you place on a friend or the same value you would place on your mother?

When you place that same high value on yourself—the kind of value you place on someone you love dearly—you begin to own your worth. You'll do whatever it takes to maintain and honor that level of value. That's where true self-worth begins: giving yourself the same energy, love, and commitment that you would give to someone you deeply respect and cherish, like your mother.

This is how you start to truly own your value—by recognizing that you are just as worthy of love, respect, and sacrifice as those you hold dear. Imagine this: you're struggling to see your own worth, your own potential. You may say things like, "I don't have this," or, "I'm not capable of that." But if I were there to guide you, I'd have to tell you we're going to disagree.

Because when I look at you, when I speak to you, when I'm around you, I see things you can't yet see in yourself. You may be so conditioned by your past experiences, your limiting beliefs, that you've tuned out the brilliance and strength that have always been within you.

Step back and consider what you've accomplished. Many people would have remained stuck in the hole you once found yourself in. But you didn't. You not only survived that place—you climbed out of it. For years, you've risen beyond what you once believed was possible. Today, you're standing stronger than ever, more aware of what you want and how to pursue it.

Now, the challenge is to put the same value on yourself and your relationships. Know what you deserve, and refuse to settle for anything less. If someone doesn't honor your worth, don't waste a second on them. Keep moving forward with the confidence and clarity that you are worthy of the best.

If I could, I'd take my eyes and let you see yourself the way I see you. If you could view yourself through my lens, the light around you would be so bright, it would take your breath away. You'd open your eyes in awe and say, "Is that really me?" And I would tell you, "Yes, that is you."

It's all a matter of perspective. I don't see your flaws. I don't focus on the things that weigh you down. I see someone who has risen above every obstacle, someone who never stops pushing forward. I see patience, strength, humility, and relentless determination. That person is you—one of the most valuable people on this planet. It's time for you to see yourself the same way.

Think about where you are right now. You may have been through unimaginable struggles—abuse, hardships, pain. Those experiences have shaped your reality, haven't they? They've kept you feeling trapped, maybe even convinced you that you belong in that hole. But listen closely: that pain does not own you anymore.

I see you. You've been through hard things, just like I have. Our situations may not be exactly the same—our beliefs, our lives, our stories might be different—but one thing is certain: we've both been in that dark place. We know the same feelings of despair, disappointment, and struggle. I've been there with you, and maybe, in some ways, we're still there together.

But here's what I want you to know: your struggles are not meant to be your shackles. You are not defined by your pain or the abuse you've faced. Those experiences don't get to hold you down forever. Your struggles are meant to build you up, to make you stronger, to show you the way forward. God didn't place you in that hole to leave you in bondage. The second you start climbing out, you begin your journey to freedom.

You are not meant to stay in the darkness. You are not meant to live a life where your past holds you captive. You are meant to rise, to climb out of that pit, and start walking toward the life you were created to live. No matter how deep the hole feels right now, it is not your final destination.

Your struggles? They don't own you. Your pain? It doesn't define you. What defines you is what you choose to do next. Will you stay stuck in that place, or will you take that first step toward the light?

Here's the truth: the journey out of the hole doesn't start when you're already at the top—it starts with that very first step. That moment when you decide, I am worth more. I am not staying here.

I know it's hard. I know it feels impossible sometimes. But I also know that you have the strength to rise. Because if you've been through the pain and the darkness and survived it, then you have the power to move beyond it. You are not a victim of your circumstances—you are a survivor. And now it's time to be a thriver.

The next step is yours. Start climbing.

So, What's Next?

Maybe your struggle involved a person in your life. At some point, you survived the abuse—you made it through. Maybe, as you grew older, as a teenager or young.

CHAPTER 11

FEAR ISN'T YOUR MASTER

Fear can keep you captive for the rest of your life. But only if you make it your master instead of your servant.

Imagine walking down a street that becomes very dark, maybe through the woods or on a lonely road. You feel fear—should you keep going, or should you turn around? Then suddenly, your flashlight beams a bright light, revealing that there's nothing there but a normal road. It was just dark. Now that you have a light, you can see clearly and walk that path without any problems, without any issues.

But what if tomorrow, you face that very same road again, and this time, you have no light? Would you be afraid? No, because you remember walking it yesterday—it was safe, nothing happened to you. So today, even without the light, you trust your steps. You could even walk it blindfolded and still feel secure.

Overcoming fear means facing it. Fear can come from a place deep in your pain, from the struggles you've faced in the hole. There is a lot to be fearful of. But remember the fear you had of never getting out? Compare that fear with the fear of getting out. Which is better? Would you rather stay in that dark place, or try something new, something better? No matter what, trying is always the better option. You already know what's down there. You already know the darkness. Now, you want to see what's above.

There is nothing more frightening than being stuck in a hole. But no matter what is waiting for you above ground, it can't be worse, and it won't be worse. There's nothing up there that will make you want to end it all. Down in that hole, you think death is the only way out because there seems to be no hope, no light. But above ground—that's where miracles happen. That's where you take control. Yes, you may face fear when you're up there, but it's a different kind of fear.

HOW LEADERS MASTER FEAR...

When you're above ground, you might wonder, "What do I do now? What comes next?" But that's a natural fear, part of being human. Nobody is fearless—not even me. But I've learned how to face my fear, and that's the difference. The fear you face underground and the fear you face above ground are two different types of fear. The fear above ground won't make you want to give up. It won't push you to the brink because you've already lived through the hardest part of your life in that hole.

Once you're out, everything becomes easier—maybe not easy, but easier. The pain is less overwhelming, the circumstances are more manageable. Yes, my life was still difficult. I was still trying to catch up, trying to become the best version of myself. But nothing compared to the fear and darkness of that hole. There's nothing I've faced above ground since leaving that hole that has made me think about ending my life again.

Life is too precious. I escaped the worst part of my life, and in doing so, I realized just how valuable life is. I survived. I escaped death. Now, nothing above ground scares me. Sure, I feel fear now and then, but it's just my human mind grappling with things that don't make much sense anyway. I've learned to face those fears and move on, like a champion.

So, conquer your fear. Compare what happened below with your new life above, and you'll find relief in that difference—being underground versus being above ground.

And for those who are afraid of what it means to be above ground, afraid because they don't know what the light looks like—remember, it's okay to be afraid. But don't let that fear stop you. Step into the light, even if you don't know what's ahead. You've already faced the darkest part. Now, it's time to see what's waiting for you in the light.

FEAR MAKES YOUR MIND THE REAL PRISON

Maybe you don't even know how to walk anymore. Think of someone who's been in prison—being stuck in your own hole is like a prison in your mind. It's okay if you're afraid of what's outside of the hole. It's okay to be afraid of peace. It's okay to be afraid of freedom.

You may question your ability to survive now that you've made it out of the pit, away from your fears and shackles. Now you're above ground, but you're afraid because you have no idea what that life is like. You're hesitant, unsure, wondering if this new life could possibly be worse than the one you just escaped from.

But the answer is, absolutely not. Even if you don't know how to live or navigate your newfound freedom and happiness, it will still be a better place. No matter what, you'll have food, a place to live, and moments of joy. You'll encounter people who might smile at you, who might ask, "Hi, how are you?" You'll experience some form of love. It will not be worse than being abused, neglected, or trapped in the darkness. Now you are in a place of safety, a place to be thankful for.

If you leave that hole with a sense of thankfulness, standing on solid ground filled with gratitude for being delivered from your worst moments, you will begin to understand that life above ground is worth living. Remember, being in that hole was the worst life possible. If you've already been there, you've already lived through your hardest moments.

I lived my worst possible life before I even turned 11 years old. After that, nothing felt as hard. Everything became easier in comparison. "Hard" now just means dealing with normal life struggles, and that's just life itself. It's not being in a place where death feels like the only option. Above ground, those chains are gone, those shackles are broken. You're no longer condemned. Now, you have the choice to move forward, as slowly or as quickly, as carefully or as boldly as you want. It all becomes a choice.

Learning to live above ground is nothing compared to being stuck in a place where you felt condemned to death.

FACING YOUR FEARS CHANGES EVERYTHING

Let's use an example: the fear of a lion. I'm still scared of lions to this day because they're powerful, and they could kill me—that's what I've always been told. The concept is simple: lions are dangerous, so I fear them. But let's say I go to a petting zoo, and they happen to have a lion. This lion has been there for many years, loved by everyone who visits. I don't know this lion; I just came with a friend who said, "Let's go to the zoo." And suddenly, there it is—a lion. Of course, my immediate reaction is fear. I want to leave because, in my mind, this lion is going to eat me.

But my friend says, "No, no, it's different." Reluctantly, I approach the fence, just a little. I slowly extend my hand and then pull it back. The lion comes over and rubs his nose against the fence. I touch his nose; it's cold, and I feel something different. Then he rubs his cheek against the fence, and I touch him again.

Suddenly, I realize I'm facing my fear. This lion isn't going to eat me; in fact, it's quite the opposite. He's friendly, gentle, majestic, powerful, but not threatening—just wanting to be petted. What if I had held on to my belief that all lions will eat you?

Getting over fear involves facing it. Not every fear can be confronted directly—sometimes a lion is not in a petting zoo; you can't touch it or get close. But it's about contrasting a lion in the wild with one that is tame. You have to figure out your fears, understand them, and navigate them, learning to feel less afraid with each step you take.

Face your fears. Understand that not every fear will lead to danger. Sometimes, it's just about learning to see things differently.

In my life, I am, of course, a military man—a 22-year Army combat veteran. Combat meaning actual combat, in conflict, facing the enemy. I can tell you that when I first went into combat, I was afraid—not afraid of the enemy, I was ready to face them—but afraid that I might become a casualty of war. Because in combat, not everyone comes home alive.

But don't mistake fear for a lack of preparation. I was completely prepared. Still, there are odds—unknowns that you can't measure or train for. The odds are that some of us would not make it back alive. That was the practical reality. Some of my friends didn't make it home. So, I found myself facing the terror of wondering, "What if I am one of those guys who doesn't make it back?"

Obviously, as a soldier, you don't dwell on these thoughts. They don't stop you from fighting or representing your country. It's what we do— it's the life we chose. But something within me said, "You know what, Alan? You've been in your hole. You've been in that dark place. You've been through all that thick darkness, and guess what? You're not going to come here, represent your country, fight for freedom, and do all the great things that we do as defenders of America just to die."

I told myself, "I am not dying today. I will survive. I will do my job, and I will do it well. And I will survive." And guess what? I made it through those hotspots—we call them battle zones. And today, I am still writing, still here, still above ground. My fear of dying wasn't as strong as my desire to live. I wanted to live, not die, and because my higher power was focused on living, not dying, I survived. I am here today, living above ground.

FINDING LIFE IN DEATH ALLEY

Let me tell you a story about walking on the battlefield—a place called Death Alley. It was where American forces and our allies bombed the area because the enemy used it to escape. All of our guns were focused on Death Alley.

Later, much later, as we swept through the battle-torn land, the noise was deafening. And I thought being in my hole was the worst thing that could ever happen to me, but it was nothing compared to this— walking through a place that had been bombed by ships, aircraft, and helicopters. Bodies were everywhere. You would want to puke, you would cry, you would have nightmares.

This is the price of war. It's the price of freedom. It's the cost of setting people free. This is what we train for. But let me tell you, seeing that, knowing that the battle wasn't over, and realizing I would have to go back into the same action again, I was scared out of my mind. Because that could have been us. The enemy had all the same equipment we did—they had big guns, they were well-equipped. We were just better, and we had air superiority that they didn't have. But I was scared. I became afraid of dying because I saw so many soldiers from the enemy's side, torn apart, pieces everywhere. It was gruesome. And every soldier, I assure you, felt that fear.

As I walked through the aftermath of the battlefield—through all the bombing and gunfire, through what was left of the enemy—I faced a choice. You always have options, though not always legal ones. Some soldiers might want to retreat or go back because what they saw was too much to bear. For a first-time combat soldier, seeing this is unlike anything you've ever witnessed before.

I could have gone back after what I'd seen, back to the bunker, faked an injury, and been taken off the battlefield. But I had to face my fear. Because of that, I was awarded the Bronze Star Medal and, most notably, the Legion of Merit. Why? Because I didn't turn back. I didn't pretend. I didn't let fear define me.

I faced my fear and continued moving forward, and that made all the difference. No matter what your fear is, facing it will take most of the edge off of it.

I had moments when thoughts crossed my mind that what I was seeing was way too much for me to handle. I never imagined it would be like that. I was someone who, at one point, craved war—I wanted to go; I volunteered to be on the battlefield. But seeing the bodies and death all around me put me into a whole new mindset. Still, I did not turn back. I faced my fear.

And what came from facing my fear was amazing. Not only did I earn the Bronze Star and the Legion of Merit, but I also became an officer. All these experiences set me up for the next part of my life, just by facing and overcoming my fears.

FEELING FEAR VS LIVING BY FEAR

I didn't let my fear dictate your actions. My actions were louder than my fear. These actions led me to not only earn all of these awards but also to become the leader who guided other men through their own fear. I was afraid—totally afraid. But I had a choice. I could have pretended, played dead, or acted like something was wrong with my foot just to get out. But then I thought, "No." I realized it was me vs myself, me vs my fear, and me vs the universe. And I decided to stand my ground.

I thought to myself, "I've survived this far. I've witnessed the reality of war, and I know I will get through this. I will reach the other side. We'll go into more battles, we'll fight more, but I am not destined to die now. God has a bigger purpose for my life." You have to believe that you are one of those people whose time has not yet come, that you will do your job to the best of your ability, no matter what. Stay sharp, protect yourself, fight well, fight fast, fight fiercely—but remember, today is not your day to die. And it wasn't mine.

I have been on the battlefield, and I am here today, writing about it. I am still above ground. From the essence of my deep pains many years ago as a child below, to now, as a grown man with hundreds of experiences and countless close encounters with death—I am here today to share the good news: I am still above ground.

I know for a fact that I have been protected. I am being protected. The angels are protecting me. My God is protecting me. The universe loves me. I am here, and so are you. We are still here, still above ground. We are meant to be here. We have a purpose, and we can get through this—together.

It's time to Face Your Fear and Move Forward

Right now, I want you to pause and get real with yourself. What is the fear standing between you and the life you want? What's keeping you trapped in that hole? Take a moment—*name it, write it down, face it directly.*

What does your fear look like? Maybe it's fear of failure, fear of rejection, or fear of not being good enough. Maybe it's the fear that things will never change. Whatever it is, write it down. Don't let it live silently in the shadows—bring it into the light.

Now that you've named your fear, I need you to ask yourself: *How do I move through this?* How do you, just like I did, embody the strength of a soldier walking across the battlefield—moving forward even when fear whispers at every step?

Find Courage Through Action

Here's the thing about fear: it only controls you as long as you let it. One of the most powerful ways to overcome fear is through action— and stories have a way of showing us how.

Let me tell you a story from one of my favorite books, "Who Moved The Cheese."

Imagine a big chunk of cheese sitting out in the open, and all the mice are happily nibbling away. They eat and enjoy the feast, day after day, until one day the cheese is gone. And suddenly, the mice are left confused, wondering, *What happened?* They never stopped to think the cheese would run out. Now they're stuck—unless they choose to go out and find new cheese.

The lesson here is simple: *If you want to survive, you have to act.* Fear can't hold you back when you take action. The mice who stay frozen in fear, hoping the old cheese will return, starve. The nice who go looking for new cheese, live and thrive. They benefit from acting in the face of fear.

How do you use fear to support YOU?

Maybe your fear right now is that your business is failing, and you don't have any new clients. It feels like a wall you can't break through—a fear that whispers, *What if it all falls apart?*

Here's what I want you to understand: *that fear is just a story.* It's not reality. It's an illusion meant to keep you trapped where you are.

But you have the power to change the story.

What happens if, instead of freezing in fear, you take new actions? What if you step outside your comfort zone, try something different, and refuse to let fear dictate your next move? The truth is, the only way forward is through. Just like the mice had to go find new cheese, you have to step out into the unknown and create new results.

Let's say you're running a business and there's an issue with your customers—you're losing them. Now, losing customers is a part of doing business. It's a situation you have to both understand and have a plan to fix. It's not something that should bind you or be a shackle. It's certainly not a showstopper. You need to take quick, decisive action to improve the situation and attract more customers.

The question is, what are you doing to attract new customers? Why are you losing customers? Maybe it's an issue with frequency—maybe you aren't delivering the way you should. If it's a restaurant, maybe the food isn't up to standard. If it's a service business, maybe the quality is slipping. If you make something, whatever it is, you first need to figure out why you're losing customers.

Ask yourself, "Why are my customers leaving? What is driving them away?" It could be the economy—perhaps it's getting tougher out there, and people are cutting back. But then, consider this: if the economy is the issue, why is it that your business specifically is affected? Is your marketing still strong? Are you still trying to attract customers?

In business, you can never stop attracting new customers or promoting your business. It's a constant, everyday effort. No one customer stays forever. They buy something, and at some point, they move on to something else or someone else. You always have to be in the motion of recruiting—recruiting doesn't necessarily mean talking to someone one-on-one; it can mean advertising, marketing, and getting your business out there.

Ask yourself: How are you doing this? What is your market? What strategies are you using? The point is, you have to face the reality of these challenges every single day. And remember, it's not a fear—it's just the way business works.

Once you understand that losing customers is a normal part of running a business, your mindset moves from fearful, to proactive. You will lose customers—that's a given. It happens in every business. In my own business, I've lost customers too, but it wasn't because they didn't like something; it's because they had spent enough money with me and moved on. So, it's up to you to keep advertising, keep getting the word out, stay on top of things to the best of your ability, and keep attracting new customers.

If you feel like nothing is happening, ask yourself why. Maybe you're saying, "I'm losing clients, so I'm afraid." But what's really happening is that you're afraid of going out of business. What I'm saying is, recognize that fear for what it is. Understand it, and then focus on the actions you can take to overcome it.

HOW ACTION DRIVES OUT FEAR

When a person decides to be proactive, they are actually facing their fear, and that's a good thing. Fear is a natural part of running a business—it's okay to have it. Without fear, you wouldn't be human. Fear is present in every aspect of your business, but don't let it paralyze you. Instead, think outside the box. Ask yourself: How do I solve this problem with my customers? What steps do I need to take?

Being proactive means taking action to get more customers. If you wait around, thinking customers will just come to you, you're missing the point. You can't afford to be passive. Keep going. This is just the beginning. You might feel stuck for a moment, and that's okay. It's a temporary feeling. Recognize that it's the fear of losing your business that's making you feel this way. But if you take immediate action, you can turn things around.

Remember, proactive actions help you face your fear—they eliminate fear. You confront your fear by dealing with it head-on. Here's the key: if you don't face your fear, that fear will keep you stuck in the hole. You have to choose—do you face it or not?

If you're fearful or uncertain about the future of your business or your career, you have to take action. Don't wait for things to reach a critical point. Start being proactive now. Look for different ways to attract customers. Once you do, the fear of losing your business will start to fade away.

Fear is just an alert system, a signal that you need to look more closely at what's happening with your customers. It's not fear in the sense of something to be scared of—it's a signal to your brain, to your senses, to your business, telling you, "We need more customers." That's all it is. But too often, people take that signal as a sign of doom, thinking, "I'm so scared; I'm afraid of losing everything." No. The universe is just nudging you to strategize, to find new ways to work with and attract customers.

It's easy to feel like the world is crashing down, but it's usually just a simple thing you need to address. People often get stuck because they can't see the beginning from the end. They think, "Oh my God, it's over." But it's not over. Far from it! Maybe you just need to hire some people, make some adjustments, or explore new strategies.

It's not over yet. You still have time. Don't give up before you've even started. Be proactive, face your fear, and take the necessary steps to keep moving forward.

Fear doesn't have to be the end of the story—it can be the beginning of a new one.

You've named your fear. Now it's time to act. Take one step, even if it's small. What can you do today that moves you closer to the life you want?

The battlefield might feel intimidating, but just like a soldier, you walk forward *despite* fear. And with every step, fear loses its grip. Because here's the truth: fear only wins if you let it.

This is your moment. The fear you've been holding? It's just a story. And you get to write a new one.

Here are two things you can do right now...:

1. Write down your fear. Identify it, name it, and acknowledge what it is.

2. Write down the actions you can take to move through that fear instead of staying shackled by it.

Ask yourself what actions can you take that will help you overcome the fear? What steps can you take right now to face it head-on? Find these, take action, and fear will flee from you.

CHAPTER 12

YOUR MOST DIVINE POWER

Faith isn't something you think about when life is easy. It's what you hold on to when everything falls apart.

When I found myself trapped in my darkest hole, I had no idea what the future held for me. And honestly, none of us ever really knows, do we? That's why faith matters so much—you have to believe in something greater than yourself, especially when the weight of your struggles feels unbearable.

But that's the thing—none of us ever really knows what's coming next, do we? And that's exactly why you need faith. You have to believe in something bigger than yourself, something greater than the pain you're feeling right now.

If you're anything like me, you might feel that pull toward a higher power—a Creator, a God, something divine that made you, shaped you, and placed love at your core. I know, without a doubt, that I was created out of love. And because of that, I believe—no, I know—that God would never just leave me behind, even when the rest of the world already had.

When everything around you feels like it's falling apart, who do you turn to? When no one picks up the phone—your mother, your father, your sister—who do you call? For me, it was a simple, desperate plea: "God, please help me out of this place."

When faith began to stir in my heart, I realized something...

Maybe the only friend I had left was my God—the One I serve. That's when things started to shift.

THE TRUE ROLE OF FAITH

Faith doesn't guarantee certainty, but it gives you something solid to hold on to. You still don't know how long the struggle will last, but you know you won't stay in that place forever. Because deep down, you trust that God—the only One who truly knows your heart—won't abandon you. And with that belief, you keep going. You keep trying. You keep crying. You keep doing everything you've been doing, but now with the unshakable faith that one day, things will change.

I started praying when I was just nine years old. Even then, I knew I needed to get out of the hole I was in. I didn't have answers, but I had faith. I knew, without a doubt, that life would change—I just didn't know how or when. But faith gave me the strength to hold on until it did.

And one day, a lady, we called Aunt Tina, came into my world. She said, "Allan, I know your grandmother." I was shocked and replied, "You know my grandmother?" She said, "Yes, she lives just a few miles down the road. I'm going to talk to her and see if she could take you in." At that moment, I felt a surge of hope: "Oh my God, you mean

I could leave this place, get out of this hole, and live with someone else?" She said, "Yes, I will pray about it and go see her."

THAT MOMENT CHANGED EVERYTHING

My faith became my lifeline. I realized that the only true friend I had, the only one I could count on, was God. Who else could have orchestrated this? I had no idea this was coming. Who was conducting this universal move to get me from where I was to where I needed to be? It had to be something much greater than the people who hated or abused me. I decided to hold on to that faith.

When she left, I kept thinking, "Will she come back? Is this real? Could it really happen?" Even if it wasn't about faith in God, I believed in that person and what she said she would do. I had my concerns, but I held on to hope that it would happen. And that's what you have to do too. You have to have faith, even if it means trusting in the unknown. You have to believe there is a path out of your pain, out of your darkness, and toward something better.

I didn't ask her to help—she came to me voluntarily and said, "I am going to do this for you." In that moment, belief and faith became intertwined. I believe—I have faith—that this person will deliver the message to my grandmother. I believe she will come back with good news, saying, "Your grandmother said yes—she's going to take you in."

I stayed faithful, waiting for that answer. Belief and faith are two sides of the same coin, but faith runs deeper. Faith is blind—it's a trust in something you have no tangible proof will happen. But still, you hold onto it. You believe so strongly—you have faith. I believed that my grandmother would say yes, even when there wasn't any certainty. Faith whispered, "I believe," even when I couldn't see how things would turn out.

Aunt Tina came into my life promising to pray for me and speak to my grandmother, bringing more than just words—she brought hope. That same faith and belief are what I hold onto. Faith is belief, but at a higher level—a deeper, more spiritual, more powerful, and more enduring level. When you truly have faith, there is a shift. Faith is belief with conviction—a conviction that transcends doubt and fear. This is what I experienced as that nine-year-old boy.

A MONTH LATER, I GOT THE NEWS...

"Your grandmother is coming to get you."

Who do you thank for that? You might thank the person who delivered the message, but who do you truly give all the praise to? It's to your one true friend who visited you while you were in that hole—your God. He cleared that path for you. You have to start believing that there is a better life for you, that He wants you to be in a much better place than you are today. This is not your destiny. You were placed in a situation by forces of evil, but you do not belong there.

You have to get past it; you have to get out of it. Once you get a taste of life outside that hole and realize the sky's the limit, you must keep believing and moving forward.

I remember thinking, "I must keep going, faithfully, because all it took was believing, even when I had no idea where I was going." And that was when the miracle happened—when the angel woman helped me escape abuse and live with my grandmother.

Think about that—do you see the magic, in the power in believing, in having faith, and staying faithful? It is here and only here where we see miracles unfold.

You have to understand what faith is. Even if you don't speak about Jesus or God, maybe you think of faith as a universal energy or spiritual force that propels you from one level to the next. If you're spiritual, it's easy to talk about faith. If you're not spiritually inclined, maybe you're open to believing in a universal power.

Believing in someone—a person of flesh and bone—to deliver a message is one thing. But having faith that there is a universal power, a God who never lies and always fulfills His promises, takes belief to another level entirely. This Faith doesn't leave room for uncertainty. It's not about wondering if the message will be delivered; it's knowing, deep in your soul, that it will be.

This is the higher level of belief I'm talking about—faith that you will be delivered from your situation. But it doesn't have to start there. Start slowly. Start by saying to yourself, "I believe she will come through for me. I believe the message will be delivered." Let that belief settle in. And over time, belief will begin to grow into something deeper. One day, you'll feel it shift: "I have faith. I have faith that I will be delivered from this situation."

When you reach that point, it's no longer just belief—it's faith. Faith goes beyond the mind; it's something spiritual and profound. It anchors you in the certainty that, no matter how things look right now, everything will work out. Faith isn't just hoping—it's knowing. It's maintaining that deeper trust, the kind of trust that says: One way or another, there is a way forward.

Whether through belief or faith, the key is to hold on. Hold on to the conviction that, one way or another, what is meant to happen will happen. And when you do, you'll find that belief—and faith—will carry you through.

Understanding the spiritual meaning of faith isn't always easy. When I was young, I didn't fully grasp it myself. Aunt Tina would tell me, "Have faith in me. I'm going to talk to your grandma and get you out of this house." And I believed her. In those moments, I held on to her words like a lifeline, even when I couldn't see how it would happen.

Over time, she taught me that the highest level of belief is faithfulness—a deep trust that goes beyond what you can see or understand. And eventually, I came to realize just how true that is. Faith isn't just about believing—it's about staying faithful, even when the path ahead is unclear. That is the kind of faith that pulls you out of the darkness and moves you toward the light.

TURNING BELIEF INTO FAITH

Take a moment to reflect on what you believe and what you have faith in. Use the prompts below to guide you:

"I believe _____ will happen."

(Example: "I believe I will find peace," or "I believe things will improve.")

"I have faith _____."

(Example: "I have faith that I will rise above my circumstances," or "I have faith that I am not alone.")

The goal here is to help you bridge the gap between belief and faith. As you fill in these blanks, notice how your belief begins to shift into something deeper—faith. This is a way to train your mind and heart to trust in things you may not yet see.

CHAPTER 13

BELIEVING FAITHFULLY - THE BRIDGE TO A BETTER LIFE

My only option when I was in the hole was to believe—to have faith. My faith had to be so strong that it could draw someone toward me, like a magnet pulling in help from the outside world. I had to believe that somehow, my silent cry would reach someone, somewhere.

I prayed: *"God, please, let someone hear me. Let someone come by—maybe someone looking for their dog—someone who just happens to notice this hole and wonders, 'Is someone down there?'"* And in my heart, I whispered, *"Yes, I'm here."*

Faith gave me the strength to believe that someone would come. I knew I couldn't afford to let disbelief take over. I had already exhausted everything—my voice, my strength, my determination—and none of it worked. But this hole wasn't my grave. It wasn't my casket.

So I prayed again: *"God, help me. I have no more strength, no more energy. You are my last resort—though you should have been my first. But now, here I am, choosing you. I need you. Only you can help me out of this."*

Even when you feel weak and buried deep in your struggle, you still have the power to choose. If you can't climb out on your own, you can choose to believe in a way out. You can choose to hold on to faith, even when everything around you feels hopeless.

FREEDOM STARTS WITH CHOICE

This is the same choice we've been talking about all along—the choice to say, *"I will not stay in this place."* Even if all you can do is whisper a prayer or send out one final cry for help, that is still a choice. It's a choice to believe that help will come, even when you have no proof.

That's what it means to have faith. It's not just about praying—it's about making the choice to hold on, even when you feel like letting go. And when the rope is lowered, when help arrives, it's about grabbing on and saying, *"Enough is enough. I'm not staying here anymore."*

When I was in the depths of my hole, I had to believe that the person who promised to come back would actually return. I had to trust that the promise would be fulfilled--that help was on the way. I needed to believe that just as someone had stumbled upon my hole, they would also help me climb out. And with that belief, a deep sense of certainty began to grow within me—I *would* be free. I *would* rise up from this hole.

So, I started smiling and celebrating my freedom before it even arrived. I sang songs to myself, whispered words of encouragement, and reminded my heart that rescue was on its way. I felt this hope deep within me—I knew that the next sound I would hear would be someone coming to pull me out.

It all starts with the choices you make in the hole. Do you choose to give up, or to believe that help is on the way? That decision shapes your outcome. When everything else has failed and you have nothing left but faith, faith becomes your lifeline. This faith gives you the strength that will eventually pull you out of the darkness.

THE FOUNDATION OF FREEDOM

Faith is not about following a set of instructions. It's not about a specific system or step-by-step process. Even the biblical prophets didn't have some rigid formula for getting to heaven. They didn't say, *"Lay bricks this way, plant a tree on the left, and you'll be saved."* Instead, they taught one powerful principle: *Believe.*

They saw faith as believing in something greater than yourself—a Creator, a force that brings order to chaos and meaning to life. They taught that belief sets you free. If you believe, you are already free. It's not about achieving perfection or checking boxes. Freedom begins the moment you believe.

You have to keep going, even when it feels impossible. You have to believe in *something.* There isn't a person alive who doesn't believe in something despite having all the details. If you believe in nothing, you begin to feel like nothing yourself. When you believe in yourself—when you connect with your purpose, your creation, and the deeper meaning of life—you'll start to feel that there's something greater keeping you in this world and giving your life purpose.

Why are you here? Why are you walking this Earth? Even in your loneliest moments, you are never truly alone. Something walks beside you, keeps you safe, and points toward a bigger picture for your life. But to discover that purpose, you must believe.

WHEN BELIEF FEELS IMPOSSIBLE

Faith is powerful because it transcends hope. With faith, you can choose to hope even when hope feels gone. This is where the struggle begins for people who don't believe in anything. People who have lost their belief often feel like they have no reason to live. Without hope, life becomes unbearably heavy.

Think back to a moment when you felt hopeless. What got you out?

Maybe you're feeling hopeless right now. Maybe you feel like there's no way out—like you can't go on. I know what that's like. I was the child who felt like his life wasn't worth living—that taking my own life was the only option.

That doesn't happen in a vacuum. When a child or an adult reaches that kind of darkness, it's often because of circumstances far beyond their control. No child just decides to end their life. Life doesn't work that way. Likewise, it's possible that you're in a hole because of things beyond your control. This might be why you feel hopeless.

But even in those darkest moments, you still have a choice. Even when you feel like the world has closed in on you, you can choose to hold on. You can choose to believe that your pain won't last forever.

There is always a bridge to freedom.

What About When You're Afraid to Hope?

If you've hoped and been let down, you might be afraid to hope again.

You might be thinking...

What choices do you have left?

So what do you do when you find yourself in such a dark place?

The answer lies in believing that something—no matter how small—can change. When you're in the hole, it's easy to feel like giving up. But faith comes from deciding that the story isn't over. Even if you can't see the way out, even if you don't feel strong enough to climb, faith says, *"This is not where I will stay."*

Your choice is to believe that help is coming. That a rope will drop. That someone will hear your cry. When that moment comes, you'll have another choice to make...

Will you grab on, or will you let it slip away?

Even if you're exhausted and bleeding, even if the climb feels impossible, you can choose to hold on and pull yourself toward freedom. Every step, no matter how painful, will bring you closer to the top. And when you reach the top—when you finally pull yourself out—you'll look back at that hole and know:

I didn't stay. I made it out.

I'm above ground.

Belief and faith are your lifelines. They remind you that, no matter how dark it gets, your story isn't over. There's always a way upward.

Sometimes, all you can see are more beatings, more hardships, more loneliness, and more deprivation. Sometimes it feels like all that will come next is more pain and suffering. That's when the dark thought creeps in...

"Maybe I do have another choice. Maybe I can leave this world."

Why would you want to leave? Because deep down, you believe there must be a better place—somewhere free from suffering, where someone will finally care for you. You start thinking, *"If I leave this world, it has to be better than what I'm going through now. Even complete nothingness would be better."* This belief does bring a strange sort of relief—because you're at least believing in something beyond the present pain.

Maybe you imagine a place where the pain will end, where you will finally be fed, finally be loved. You may end up, metaphorically speaking, lying under the wheel of that truck, waiting for it to roll over you. You may convince yourself that this is how you'll escape and find peace and finally be seen for who you are. You might believe that this is the way to live a life without the abuse and without loneliness.

You may think, *"I'll be gone. Nobody will hurt me anymore. They'll finally know who I was, and they'll see me for who I truly am."* You may surrender to this feeling, and lie under your truck wheel, waiting for the moment when your suffering will end.

But maybe—just maybe—something deep within you will whisper, *"No, not today. This isn't the way out. This is not how you escape your mission on this Earth."* Something spiritual, unseen, and yet profoundly real, tells you: *"You have to face it. You have to overcome it."*

That's when your truck driver will come. He may kick you, curse, and yell for you to get out of the way. He may drive off, leaving you still alive and breathing. You may lie there, asking, *"Why can't I just die? It would be so easy."* But maybe—just maybe—someone doesn't want you to die. Maybe, despite everything, you are here for a reason.

If you try to leave this world, and end up still here...you have a second chance, and a new choice.

What do you do now?

You realize that if you're still here, still breathing, then *you are meant to be here.* This is not the end. You have to believe that you are here for a reason—and that dying is not part of that reason.

Everything changes when you reach this moment. You understand that God did not put you on this Earth to die but to *live—fully, deeply, and with purpose.* You understand that your life has meaning, and that your story isn't over yet.

There is Always A Bridge to Purpose and Faith

Imagine if I had died at eight years old. What would the world have missed out on? Just think—if my plan had worked, and that truck had gone over my head, I would have been gone. I would have died at eight, without ever experiencing life beyond my present pain and suffering. I would have no joys, no victories, and no purpose fulfilled.

But I didn't die. I know now what the voice meant, when I heard it say...*"You are staying. You are not going anywhere."*

I am here today, writing this book—*Above Ground*—because I overcame the suffering, the pain, and the desire to leave. I now believe in a higher power—a force so vast and powerful that it has guided me from place to place, keeping me alive for the sake of my bigger purpose.

I have to believe in that purpose—and to live it.

My life has touched thousands of people. I've helped hundreds through their darkest challenges. And I can't help but wonder: *What if I hadn't made it? What if I hadn't been here to write the book you're holding right now?*

What if I had taken my life? What if I hadn't believed in something greater?

Likewise, you have to think about what will happen if you stay in your hole. Someone, somewhere, will miss out on being touched by your story. Maybe a lot of people. Maybe millions.

This is where faith and purpose go hand in hand. Purpose means that your life matters. If you're still here, there is something you're meant to do.

Something only *you* can do.

Like me, you have to believe in that purpose. You have to choose to live it. Even if you're not sure what it is.

You have to believe in something, and it's your choice what that thing will be. This choice will guide you, not only out of the hole, but in every decision you make.

As I'm writing this, I'm asking myself...

What if I had given up? What if I had decided to stop moving forward instead of transitioning from a military career to leading organizations and becoming president of various groups?

I remember the conversations...

"Allan, will you be our president?" *Yes.*

"Allan, will you join the board of dentistry?" *Yes.*

Opportunities came my way, and I accepted them. Even when opportunities didn't come right away, I knew my purpose was much bigger and I believed that opportunities were coming. All the suffering and pain I went through had prepared me for the next round–the next mission. They were molding me to care for others, to love deeply, and to teach others how to love. They were shaping me to become a champion—an ambassador of love, understanding, and compassion.

There are people out there right now who will need you to show up for them as well. Think about them when you're feeling hopeless. They will give you hope.

Think of all the men I led in the army. If I had given up, they would have missed out on my guidance. The decisions I made in the hole, helped me become the leader they needed.

WHAT MAKES A GREAT LEADER?

Is leadership something you learn in training? Do they teach you how to believe in yourself in basic training? No. It all starts in the hole, in those desperate moments when you're alone and forced to develop skills, coping mechanisms, and survival strategies.

When I grew up and served in the military, I knew I had a duty to protect the men under my command. Hundreds of soldiers counted on me, just like I once counted on someone to protect me. And because of that responsibility, I made sure that many of my soldiers came home—alive and safe—back to their families, to their parents, their wives, their spouses.

But what if I hadn't made it? What if I had accepted death as my only answer?

These questions reveal the power of choices—even choices that seem small in the moment.

Life is a series of choices, and those choices define who we are and where we go. Every day, we make decisions that shape our lives. The essence of life is not just surviving—it's about choosing who you want to be and where you want to go.

So, what message do I offer to anyone who feels like death is the only way out? What blessing can I give to those who believe there is no escape from their pain? Here it is, and I offer it with full transparency: The stories and lessons I share in this book are here for you. They exist for you to lean on, to draw strength from, and to find inspiration.

You're not alone. You have a purpose. Remember these words. Find yourself in them. Find motivation through my suffering, through my pain. At one time, I also believed that the only way out was death. I didn't just think about it—I tried it. I laid under those truck wheels, ready to give up on everything because I couldn't bear the weight of life anymore.

You might be in that same place right now. Maybe it feels like it's over, like there's no way out. But I'm telling you: *you don't have to see the way out to believe that one exists.* You just have to hold on to the idea that there is a way forward. Have faith. Believe that you are called to something greater than your pain.

When you're standing at the edge, ready to break, that's the moment you must dig in and say, *"No, not today."* That's the moment you discover your true purpose. It's when you begin to realize that leaving isn't the answer, no matter how tempting it seems.

I won't sugarcoat it—I wanted to end it all. I thought that ending my life was the only way to find peace. It seemed like the easiest way out. But I'm standing here today, writing these words to you, because I discovered that peace doesn't come through giving up—it comes through pushing forward.

But let me tell you something: if I had succeeded in ending my life, I would have missed everything that came after. I would have missed becoming the person I am today, missed living the life I now cherish, and missed touching the lives of so many people. Just this one life—*my life*—has impacted thousands of people, in ways I never could have imagined. And I had no idea it would.

But here I am—alive. And if you're feeling like you have no choice, I need you to think again.

IMAGINE YOUR LIFE ABOVE GROUND

If you're lying under that truck wheel, get up. *Get up and know that your life has purpose.* Trust me on this. Have faith that you are here for a reason, not just for yourself, but for others too. There is a much bigger calling on your life, and it's waiting for you to claim it.

When you're deep in that hole, the light feels unreachable. It's hard to see beyond the darkness, hard to imagine anything good waiting on the other side. But I want to paint a picture for you—*a picture of what freedom feels like when you follow your purpose.*

Of course, being in the depths of that hole can limit your imagination. If you haven't lived much of your life yet, you might wonder, *Is there really anything better out there? Is there any reason to keep going?* When your experience is limited, your perspective can feel just as small.

I know exactly what that feels like. When I was there, I faced two choices. I thought about drowning myself, but the thought of it dragged me down even more—it seemed too painful, too slow. So I considered a quicker way out. Even then, I had no idea what was on the other side. All I could think about was leaving—*escaping* the pain.

I saw others living their lives, smiling, being loved, and enjoying their days. None of that was happening for me. I wondered, *Could that ever be me? Could someone love me, see me, care about me?* Those questions made me pause. *Should I go now, or should I wait?*

Should I go now, or should I wait?

It's hard to see far ahead when you're stuck in darkness. But sometimes, all you need is a leap of faith—a belief that there's something better waiting, even if you can't see it yet.

Even as a child, in my darkest moments, I held on to a vision. I imagined what I could do with my life if I made it out. I wanted to serve others. I dreamed of being a healer—someone who could walk into a hospital, lay hands on the sick, pray to God, and see them rise up, fully healed. That was my deepest wish, my prayer to God. I didn't just want to heal bodies—I wanted to heal minds and souls.

You have to reach a place in your mind where you start imagining possibilities. *You are not stuck.* Your circumstances may feel heavy, but your story doesn't end in that hole. Let my story be your example.

I didn't hurt myself. I wasn't meant to die. Even in my lowest moment, when I believed there was no way out, something bigger than me whispered: *"Not today."*

And that was enough.

I never tried again. Running away from that truck alive, I realized something important: *I still had life. I still had choices. I still had a chance.* That realization gave me momentum to keep moving, to figure things out, and to stay alive. I chose to live—and to fight for another day.

TODAY IS YOUR DAY TO LIVE!

If you're reading this now, I need you to hear me: *Today is not your day to leave.* No... TODAY IS YOUR DAY TO LIVE!!

No matter how dark it feels right now, *Today is your day to live.* You have a choice—just like I did. And with that choice comes a purpose, one far greater than you can imagine right now. Hold onto that purpose. Even if you can't see the way out yet, believe that it exists. Your story doesn't end here.

Get up. *Live.* Your best days are waiting for you.

Remember when I told you the story about almost drowning? How, in the midst of abuse and hopelessness, I didn't believe that God was there? You might feel the same way right now—just as I did back then.

I had fAllan off the tube, sinking deeper and deeper into the water, convinced it was over. We were so far out, so deep, that I thought I was done. I kept sinking, hands flailing, paddling desperately through the water, searching for anything to grab onto. But there was nothing.

Then, out of nowhere, something brushed against my hand—a piece of cloth. My eyes burned from the salty water, so I kept them shut, but I clung to that cloth with everything I had. As it turned out, it was the shorts of another swimmer who was still on the tube. They pulled me up—back to the surface, back to life. In that moment, I knew, without a doubt, that God had a purpose for me. There was no way that was just chance; it was a miracle. I had been slipping deeper and deeper, ready to disappear, and suddenly, someone happened to be there, and I found my way to them—even with my eyes closed. That wasn't luck. That was God.

That moment reminded me that there is a higher power at work—a force that intervenes, even when we can't see it. And just like in that moment, you have to believe that your life is not a coincidence. You're not meant to leave this world. You have a purpose. Your life has meaning.

LIVING IS YOUR RESPONSIBILITY

You're *not* meant to take your life. Your responsibility is to live, to share your experiences, to give love, and to help others find their way. That is your superpower: *to live.*

If you're having thoughts of ending your life, I want to offer you something practical—a way forward, starting with your imagination. Right now, you might be using your imagination to picture how you'll escape the hole through death, thinking that leaving is your only way out. But what if we changed that vision? What if, instead of imagining death, you imagined life?

Take a moment. Take a deep breath. Picture yourself at the top of this hole, standing in the sunlight. Picture a version of your life where the pain has lessened, where you feel lighter—even if just for a moment. Visualize the places you want to go, the people you want to love, and the things that bring you joy. Imagine your dog, your cat, or the sound of birds singing in the morning. Picture yourself surrounded by smiles, warmth, and peace. What does that life look like?

When I was in my darkest place, I began to do the same thing. I saw people, I saw smiles, and I imagined myself sitting at a table filled with food, sharing moments of joy. And just like that, I felt a flicker of life stir within me. The vision was so simple, yet it gave me something to hold onto. Even though I was still deep in the hole, that glimpse of what could be—of what *was possible*—was enough to make me feel alive for just a moment.

And when the darkness tried to pull me back, when I felt hope slipping away, I remembered that vision. That picture of life was more powerful than any thought of death. I realized then that I didn't really want to die—I wanted to live the life I had just seen in my mind. I wanted that better something. I wanted to get out of that hole and live.

THIS IS YOUR WAY OUT...

So, here's what I ask of you: Paint that picture for yourself. Imagine the life you want to live—the life that's waiting for you beyond the pain. Hold onto that vision, even if it feels far away. Let it become your way out.

The choice to live starts in your mind, with the images you create and the belief you hold. It's okay if you can't see the whole picture yet—just start with a small glimpse. Picture *one good thing* and let it grow. That vision is your lifeline.

Because even when everything feels dark, even when you think the only way out is to leave, I promise you—there is more waiting for you. Your story doesn't end here. Your life still has so much to give. And your purpose? It's not to leave. *It's to live.*

CHAPTER 14

THE GREATEST OF ALL FREEDOMS

Life doesn't come with a clear, step-by-step guide. There's no formula that says, "Step one: run fast. Step two: slow down. Step three: jump three steps. Step four: run faster, then stop." That's not how life works. It's unpredictable, messy, and unique to each of us. And the purpose of this book is not to give you rigid instructions—it's to teach you to believe in yourself, to have faith in things you never thought possible, and to see your life from a new perspective.

Perspective is everything.

For example, I spent only 48 hours of my life with my mom. That's it. Just two days. And one day, a friend came to me, drowning in grief, saying, "I lost my mom after 32 years. I feel sad, depressed, and even suicidal."

I sat with her at that moment and said, "You had 32 years with your mom. How beautiful that must have been! How fortunate you were to have all that time together." Then I shared my story. "I only had 48 hours with my mom."

As she reflected on that, something shifted within her. She started to see her own life differently. "Why am I suicidal? Why am I so depressed?" she asked herself. Here I was—someone she looked up to, someone she saw as successful, happy, and thriving—yet I had only two short days with my mother. She began to realize how blessed she had been to have 32 years of love and memories.

I told her, "Look at me—I am smiling, I am happy, and I am here talking to you about moving forward, even though I had only two days with my mom. I didn't even meet her until I was 24 years old, and when I finally did, we only had two hours together. But you—you had your entire childhood with her. You were rocked, loved, kissed, and cherished for 32 years."

Through that conversation, I was able to help her climb out of her hole—not by fixing her grief, but by offering a new perspective on her situation. My experience, as difficult as it was, became the ladder she needed to pull herself out.

BECOME SOMEONE'S LADDER OF HOPE

Once you learn how to climb out of your own hole, you have a new responsibility: to become a ladder for someone else. Just as I helped her by sharing my story, it becomes your responsibility to do the same for others. You've been through pain, you've taken the steps toward healing, and now you understand the journey in ways only someone who has walked it can. That experience gives you the power to guide others who are still struggling.

So how do you help someone else who is stuck in their own darkness? You start by going back to your own experience. Ask yourself:

- What pain was I in?

- How did I feel?

- What did that pain do to me?

- How many times did I cry out from hunger, loneliness, or feeling unloved?

By revisiting your own story, you connect with the emotions and struggles that others are going through. And from that place of understanding, you can offer them something invaluable: hope.

The beauty of becoming a ladder for others is that you don't have to be perfect or have all the answers. You just have to show them that it's possible to move forward—that life, even with its hardships, is still worth living.

Maybe your faith was stronger, and you were able to understand things without anyone intervening. Maybe God was there for you in those moments, connecting with you spiritually. But the person you're helping may not have had that opportunity—they may not know faith or God in any way. This might be their chance to learn, to discover that there is a bigger universe, a greater spirituality at work.

Your role is to help them out of the predicament they're in. Start with belief—not necessarily using the word "faith" just yet. It begins with the simple thought: *"I will be free from this hole. I believe I will not be stuck here forever. The One who created me would not leave me here. What would be the purpose of my existence if it were only pain and sorrow with no end in sight? At some point, it has to change, and I believe that it will."*

Help them to keep praying, keep hoping, and keep their faith strong. Remind them to hold tight to their belief that someone will come along, that a rope or ladder will be lowered, and that they will climb out. You help them remember to cling to the hope that their freedom is coming.

If you yourself are still stuck in the hole, find others who have been through the same hole, ask them, "How long did it take you to get out? Was it painful?" Let yourself feel hope when they share their story with you.

For me, getting out of my hole took time. My hole was deep, and I was only a child when I fell into it—but I climbed out. And I am no longer in that place.

One thing you long for when you're trapped in that hole is *freedom*—the freedom to make your own choices. It may seem like there are no choices when you are stuck, but choices are always there. Now, everyone reading this is likely an adult, with the power to make better choices and seek a better life. We all have the ability to do that, just like I did.

When I came to America, I was on my own. My family got me here, then told me, "Figure it out." And that's exactly what I did. It was a different world, full of opportunities, and for the first time, I began to truly live—not just survive or go through the motions. I no longer just wanted to wake up, repeat the same routine, and go back to sleep. No, I now wanted to live and enjoy every single day.

So, I focused on improving myself daily, because I knew one thing for certain: I never wanted to go back to that hole.

I took deliberate steps to better myself, to find that place where my happiness meets me—or where I meet my happiness. And I kept moving forward, step by step.

YOU ARE STILL IN CONTROL

Let me remind you that the fact that you are alive today means that you, too, are no longer trapped in that hole. When you recognize that, you realize that life is held within your hands.

If you choose to stay where you are, that's your decision. If you choose to move forward, that's your choice too. You have the freedom to decide which direction you take—whether you go left, right, or forge a brand-new path entirely.

When life becomes a series of choices that you make, the shackles are gone. The power is in your hands. You might feel overwhelmed and think, *"I don't know what to do."* But ask yourself: "Do I want to go back to where I was?"

No, you don't. So now, the question becomes: *What will you do differently to avoid slipping back into that place? What choices can you make today to move forward, toward the life you want?*

It all comes down to this—you *do* have a choice. You have the power to change your path.

You have a choice: to stay in the hole or to climb out of it. I know it might feel like there is no choice—that you're trapped with no way out. But let me tell you something important: "You HAVE choice." You have agency—the power to make decisions for yourself. Agency means recognizing that the path forward is in your hands.

Imagine yourself in a deep hole, desperately trying to climb out. You push, you claw, and every time you take a step up, you slip right back down. No matter how hard you try, you keep falling. But you don't give up—you keep going. You push yourself until, eventually, you realize something important: *What you're doing isn't working.* You need more than just effort. You need something different. You need help.

Then, a kind woman walks by and looks down at you in the hole. They ask, *"Why are you down there?"* You reply, *"I can't get out."* The person responds, *"I can help."*

Here's where your first real choice appears. *Do you accept the help, or do you say, "No, I'm fine. I love being here. I'll figure it out on my own"?* Maybe at first, you're reluctant. You think to yourself, *I don't need help—I've got this.* So, you keep trying. Day after day, you climb and fall, climb and fall, but nothing changes. You're still stuck, still deep in the same place.

A few days or weeks pass, and the woman returns. She looks down at you and asks, *"Are you still down there?"* You nod and say, *"Yes, I'm still here."* She asks again, *"Do you need help?"*

This time, something shifts. You realize that you've tried everything you could, but you can't do it alone. You have to decide: *Will I stay in this place, or will I accept the help I've been offered?*

And this time, you look up and say, *"I want to go. Will you help me?"*

The woman leaves for a few hours and returns with a thick, sturdy rope. She ties it securely to a tree and calls down to you, *"Can I lower this rope to you?"*

Here's another choice—yes or no. This time, you say, *"Yes."* She drops the rope down to you, and you face one more decision: *Do I grab onto the rope and climb out, or do I tell her, "Never mind, pull the rope back up. I'll stay here a bit longer and figure it out myself"?*

But this time, you've made a decision. You grab the rope. *Enough is enough.* You make the decision: *I'm not staying in this place any longer.*

You start to climb. Your hands bleed, your feet scrape against the jagged walls of the hole, but you don't care. You see the blood, but all you feel is the thrill of liberation—the rush of breaking free. You climb higher, closer to the top, driven by the belief that freedom is within your grasp.

And finally, your hand reaches the edge, then your other hand. You pull yourself up, one foot at a time, until you're standing at the top. You made the choice to get out, and you did it—with a little help.

You stand there, breathing deeply, looking down at the hole you just escaped. At that moment, what would you say? What would you do? Maybe you'd shout to the sky, thanking whatever higher power you believe in. Maybe you'd whisper a quiet prayer of gratitude for the strength to climb out.

CHOOSE LIFE, OR CHOOSE DEATH

Every day is a choice to move toward life, or toward death. There are no in betweens. What matters most is this: *You made the choice to get out. You chose to believe that this is not where you were meant to stay.*

Even when you're at your lowest, you still have choices. You can choose to cry and lament that you're stuck, or you can choose to strategize, to pray, and to find new ways forward. You can choose to hold onto hope, believing that a rope will be lowered and that someone will come to help you out of that place. And when that help arrives, you can choose to accept it.

Being in the hole doesn't mean you're weak. It doesn't matter how brave or strong you think you are—being in that place can still make you feel powerless. But there is strength to be found even in the darkness. Strength comes from the choices you make, no matter how small.

Your power lies in the choices you make from here. *Will you stay in the darkness, or will you climb toward the light?*

I took deliberate steps to better myself, to find that place where my happiness meets me—or where I meet my happiness. And I kept moving forward, step by step. The fact that you are alive today means that you, too, are no longer trapped in that hole. Now it's in your hands.

You have the freedom to decide which direction you take—whether you go left, right, or forge a brand-new path entirely.

When life becomes a series of choices that *you* make, the shackles are gone. The power is in your hands. You might feel overwhelmed and think, *"I don't know what to do."* But ask yourself: *"Do I want to go back to where I was?"*

No, you don't. So now, the question becomes: *What will you do differently to avoid slipping back into that place? What choices can you make today to move forward, toward the life you want?*

It all comes down to this—you *do* have a choice. You have the power to change your path.

You might think you don't have a choice, but you do. You have agency—the power to make decisions for yourself, no matter how impossible things might feel. Agency means realizing that even when you're in the darkest hole, the way forward is still in your hands.

CHAPTER 15

HOW TO MOVE FROM PANIC TO POWER

The hole I was locked in was truly my place of training for all my future endeavors. Without all the hardships I faced, my life just wouldn't make any sense. I wouldn't be here today—I wouldn't be the person I am now: the leader, the soldier, the father, the volunteer, the public servant, or the person running for office, confident in my leadership skills and a perfectionist when dealing with technical situations that require the utmost accuracy.

My place of horror and sorrow was not my destiny; it was merely a pause in my life, a place to become the man I am today, the leader who helps others through their own struggles and battles, making life more tolerable, fearless, and reachable for others. My dark place was not my sentence; it was my freedom, my redemption, the place where I learned humility, patience, and how to walk in faith fearlessly to become an achiever—and to inspire others to do the same.

I wrote "Above Ground," to teach you how to think, what not to think, and how to navigate life daily through faith and positive thinking. This book teaches you the principles of wisdom, faith, persistence, and overcoming adversity through a belief system, through a motivational self that clings to life and learns that living is the ultimate goal. Not just living, but living with purpose, living intentionally, staying alive, and thriving above ground.

As a life coach, I help people do this everyday. There is a collection of attributes that people may share, but my approach to life coaching is unique to each individual. Everything I do is custom-made for each client. I tailor their routines and solutions specifically for them. The things I have taught you in this book, you can start customizing your own routines and solutions.

FROM FAITH TO ACTION

We've talked about faith, belief, getting out of the hole, finding solutions, facing fear, and getting help. Now, I want to talk about action.

So, imagine you are my client. How would I guide you to take action and know what to take action on? Most of my clients, or people I coach, struggle with issues like depression. They don't smile. They aren't happy. They're in bad moods. Many times, you have to go back to the root cause and ask, "Why are you feeling this way?" It might be because they don't feel well, aren't eating right, or aren't sleeping enough. There are many causes that can push people into a depressive state. Sometimes, it's the result of a situation that is just long and extenuating, beyond the norm. But these are situations we can help with, situations we can address and manage ourselves.

How you feel and how your body reacts to certain things are often influenced by how we contribute to them. Nobody's perfect. There are many times I wake up feeling a little down or out of place, but I take a deep breath, rethink my strategy, adjust my mindset, and put a smile on my face. It's always helpful when you can wake up, smile, and take on the day.

But it's a problem when you wake up and see everything as negative. If you think, "It's Monday, it's going to be a terrible day," and go back to sleep, you're missing out on gratitude. Instead, think, "It's Monday, I'm alive, I get to see another day." Be thankful for that. If it's raining, think, "Great! My grass was already dry; we needed the rain." When you assume bad energy, you attract bad energy. But when you assume gratitude, you open a space for the divine to bless you with more to be grateful for.

I could've witnessed all the miracles that had happened in my life when I was saved from the abuse and loved by my grandma. I could've felt the power of faith and belief and simply just stayed in my home country of Jamaica.

But instead, I allowed my mindset shifts to propel me forward in action. And that action led me to a life of leadership.

Being in my hole taught me a lot about leadership. Everything I carried forward into my life above ground was what I learned in that hole. Leadership became my most valuable skill throughout my career. Even today, my ability to lead, direct, organize, stay calm, analyze situations, and find solutions is what defines me. I believe that one of my life's callings is to lead.

LEADERS ARE ACTION TAKERS

But those leadership traits were born in my younger days, when I was stuck in that hole, fighting for myself, making decisions on my own, and trying to elevate myself. When I joined the army, it didn't take long for others to notice that I was a natural leader. I was often appointed to serve in leadership positions. Everywhere I went, especially in terms of schooling, I found myself in leadership positions. In the military, I excelled, rapidly climbing the ranks—from a non-commissioned officer to a Chief Warrant Officer. Leadership was my key because it had been ingrained in me from a very young age. I learned to make decisions and stick by them, always guided by my faith in God. I became a fearless leader, blessed with the opportunity to lead men into combat and bring them all home safely, without a single casualty.

On the civilian side, after leaving the army, the first thing I did was buy a technology company and become its president. Shortly after, I joined Rotary, and within eight months, I was elected president of the club. I even flew all the way to Osaka, Japan, for a Rotary International Convention, where I learned everything I could about Rotary. I returned inspired and motivated, taking my club from 14 members to 45. Soon after, I was asked by the Chamber of Commerce board to accept the position of Chamber President, where I increased membership from about 170 to over 450 in a very short time—less than two years.

I also served as the President of the NAACP, the Assistant District Governor for Rotary, and the District Leadership Chair for Rotary. My knack for recruiting and inspiring new members to join our ranks led to me being appointed by the Governor to serve on the Board of

Dentistry, a four-year commitment. Remarkably, I was the consumer member, while all other board members were dentists or in the dental profession. I was there to protect the interests of Kentuckians and their citizens. At one point, the board needed a new president, and they asked me to serve, despite the fact that I was not a dentist. They were so captivated by my leadership that they wanted me to take on the role. I graciously declined, believing the position should be held by an actual dentist, but I promised to support the president and help in any way I could. This was just one example of how my leadership skills were sought after at the highest levels. I felt incredibly blessed and grateful that they would even consider me for such a position.

I was also recruited to run for public office as a state representative for the 26th District. Although I did not win that election, the fact that a boy who had been stuck in a hole for so long—with no hope, no life, no love, starved, beaten, and abused—could come to this country and run for public office is proof of God's blessings.

I have found that some of the best leaders lead powerfully because of the hole they had once been in... but they only could because of their inspired and fearless action. Dreams are great, talk is cheap and procrastination is a dream killer. I am a man of action which parts seas, propelled rockets to space, lands man on the moon, ships are built the size of cities that sail the open seas, submarines that sail the depth of the ocean floor. Action is where you create opportunities and possibilities, it's where your vision and dreams are realized, ideas born, action is the solution, it's what builds leaders.

CHAPTER 16

THE GIFT OF FORGIVENESS

I had never met my mom. Now, at 28 years old, I felt an urgency to meet her. I was about to be deployed for my first combat tour, the talk was serious—discussions of how cruel the war could be, the possibility of chemical or even sub-nuclear weapons. It was my first time going into combat, and like everyone else, I was scared. The unknown dangers we would face weighed heavily on my mind. But there was one thing on my mind, one thing on my bucket list: I wanted to meet my mom before I died.

At this time, I was stationed in Germany, and my mom was in England. So, I quickly came up with a plan to travel to England to see her, to meet her, to see her face for the first time. I had many questions, maybe three pages full. There were so many things I needed to know—so many "whys." I decided to take leave from Germany and travel to England to meet my mom. It wasn't a surprise; I told her I was coming, though I didn't have her exact contact information. She was living in Sheffield, England, about two hours south of London.

I decided to spend seven days with her. I drove from Germany to England, took the ferry from Dover across the channel, and continued driving on the other side. I arrived safely in Sheffield, and my mom met me at the door. She took my hands in hers, smiling the entire time. For the first time, I saw what my mom looked like. She showed me to my room, and after settling in, we hugged and talked a bit. I wasn't sure when to start asking her the questions I had come with. I had just arrived, and I wanted to enjoy the moment of seeing her face, seeing her smile, and listening to her voice.

The next day came, and I thought it would be the most appropriate time to ask her the questions that had been on my mind before I went off to combat. But that didn't happen. To be honest, my heart was full of joy just being with my mother, the person who gave birth to me. I couldn't bring myself to ask those "whys." I didn't want to change the mood. I just wanted to enjoy her company, walking through the house, being in each other's presence. We never talked about my early days or what happened when I was a baby. We just focused on the present, being together. I knew she was overjoyed to see me, and I felt the same.

But then something happened. I got a call from my unit in Germany. I was summoned back immediately because our deployment schedule had been moved up due to the escalating war. Instead of spending seven days in England, I would be leaving the very next day. I realized I would only have about 40 hours with my mom. Now I know that's probably why I never asked those "why" questions or discussed the things I had planned. And to be honest, at that moment, they didn't seem important. Time had passed, and I had moved beyond the pain and sacrifices. I just wanted to see her face. I wanted to make sure that if God took me from this Earth, I would at least have seen my mom.

FORGIVENESS = PEACE WITH YOUR PAST

There was no blame, only hope. I had never felt so warm and at peace. She actually reminded me of my grandmother in some ways. Sometimes, I felt as if I was with her instead. It was an amazing experience. Finally, I had to leave. I remember driving back to Dover, crossing the channel to get back to Germany. I wasn't sure how fast I was driving or how far I had gone. I was lost in thoughts of gratitude for seeing my mom. It could have been a better visit, but it wasn't. Yet, I was filled with love and compassion. I felt sorry, not for her, but for both of us and our situation.

Even after crossing back into Germany, the feeling never left me. I still couldn't believe that after all those years—after all the pain, suffering, and longing, asking, "Where's my mom? Mom, are you coming back for me?"—I had finally seen her face before going off to combat. I'm pretty sure if it wasn't for the combat deployment, I would never have seen her. Something deep inside me just knew that seeing her face was something I needed to do before I died.

What I didn't tell you is that my mom was married and living with her husband in Jamaica. Jamaica, being a British colony, often saw Jamaicans traveling to England to find work or improve their family's circumstances. My mom's husband decided to go to England to create a better life for his family. I wasn't born yet. While her husband was away, my mom stayed back in Jamaica, waiting for the word that she would join him.

During that waiting period, she met my father, and that's when I was born. Her husband in England knew nothing about me. When the day came that he called her and said, "Hey wifey, it's time to come," she had, I imagine, two choices: to take me with her and tell her husband about the situation or to go without me.

Both choices had consequences. If she took me with her, she would have to tell her husband she had been unfaithful and had a child. This was not something easily accepted, especially in those times—it was surely frowned upon, and she likely feared divorce. Her other choice was to leave me behind. I am certain this was another hard choice for her.

Knowing my family, I don't believe my mom was an evil woman. I believe she was kind and loving. I have to believe that her choice to leave me behind was to save her marriage or to protect her family's future. Either way, she made a choice, and I was left behind.

LETTING GO OF RESENTMENT

You might wonder why I'm not bitter. Yes, I was totally bitter growing up. I was angry all the time because I saw my friends with their moms in school, helping them, doing all the motherly things I never experienced. At 10 years old, when I heard the words "I love you" for the first time, I had to ask my grandmother what that even meant. That was painful and sad for me. I wished I had my mom during those early days, telling me all the things a mom would say. But I didn't have those experiences growing up.

As I became older and my thoughts matured, I began to understand why she didn't take me with her. I had to come to terms with it and find it in my heart to forgive her. After all, my life turned out to be amazing. My grandmother was there to provide the love, devotion, and security I needed at 11 years old. Yes, I missed the first 10 years with my mom, but I wouldn't trade my life for anything. The experiences I had helped me start to forgive my mom for leaving me behind.

Sometimes, it's strange, but I actually thank her for leaving me behind. I'm not sure who I would have been or where I would have gone if I had followed a different path, but in this life, I know who I am. I know my strengths, I know my mission.

When I went to England to see my mom, I did have questions and concerns, but there was no anger. I wanted to ask her just one thing: "Why did you leave me behind?" That was my biggest question, but it was a question I could have answered myself. I just wanted to hear it from her. I understood that her decision involved her husband and the conflicts it could cause. Was it a sacrifice? Was I the sacrificial lamb? I believe I was.

Regardless, her decision helped me grow into the person I am today— a person filled with love, joy, and a passion for saving lives and reaching out to others. I'm a father to four boys and a husband to my wife—things I learned from my grandmother, not from my mom. I had an incredible life, a great life.

Don't think that because the early years of my life were filled with trauma, beatings, depression, hunger, and a lack of basic needs, that it deterred me from my mission and God's plan for my life; that was not to be; not today, not ever!!

My dear mother, the woman I barely know, the son you haven't known, my heart was so empty now filled with joy, seeing your beauty, your smile, your touch was the miracle I needed most to heal my aching soul from our abandonment. I have missed you for a thousand years. I often wondered about this very moment, seeing you for the first time 28 years later and touching your face, hugging you without the feeling of wanting to let go. I had so many questions for you but they escaped my mind, something came over me, something so strong, so spiritually powerful, I came to you as an empty jar, I left with a thousand drums of joy, a smile you could see across the continent, finally I found peace, I found the love of my mother. My beautiful mom, now I am sad leaving you behind, off to combat not sure if I will ever feel the warmth of your embrace again. Time was short, the clock never slept, neither did I. I realized I have always loved, I just needed to find my way to you. Mother, I forgive you and I will love you forever.

FORGIVENESS FOR THE SAKE OF YOUR FUTURE

You'll never crawl out of your hole or truly find freedom if you don't let go of certain things. If you hold on to the past, you will remain shackled for the rest of your life. There were things I had to release, things I had to confront to stop being a victim. One of the most important things I had to do was deal with my situation with my mother — to forgive her, to love her.

Imagine loving someone you've never met. Imagine loving someone who brought so much pain and agony into your early years. Yes, I blamed her for that. She made a choice, and I wasn't the priority. But to move forward and align with my higher purpose, I had to let go of all that pain. It took me a long time to reach that point. I'm not going to tell you it was easy — it was hard, very hard.

The person who should have been my protector, my angel, my mother — the one everyone depends on — wasn't there for me. I couldn't believe it. I struggled to forgive and move on. The longer I held on to the resentment, the more the bitterness towards my mother grew. I felt anger consuming me, and it actually made my pain worse than when I was in the hole.

It wasn't easy for me. There were times when I cried, shouted, and screamed because of the anger I felt about what she did. In my mind, I would imagine standing in front of her, yelling and asking, "Why? Why would you do that to your own child?"

These feelings stayed with me for a long time. But once I began to understand her situation, I was able to take a step back and start healing. I began telling myself, "Mom, I love you," long before I even knew her. Believe me, that wasn't easy. But as I did, I started to feel less bitter, less angry. I set myself free through forgiveness.

Forgiveness played a major role in my life. It set me free. It released the shackles that held me down because even when I had escaped my physical hole, I was still miserable and in pain. I hadn't let go. It wasn't until I learned to accept and forgive that I could truly feel love for my mom.

That love stayed with me every single day of my life, to the point where, when I finally saw her, I didn't want to question or accuse her. I just wanted to connect with her, to hug her, and to love her unconditionally. The greatest joy I ever felt was when I saw my mom's face. The joy I felt when she touched my hands, when she hugged me, when she took me to my room and showed me where I would be staying for the next seven days. I felt like a child all over again.

FROM FORGIVENESS TO INNER PEACE

How do you let go of bitterness? No matter what you're bitter about or how hard it is, forgiveness is the key. Until you embrace forgiveness, you will remain shackled by your past. Even after escaping my darkest times, I was still unhappy because I hadn't truly forgiven my mom.

Forgiveness brings an angelic feeling, a sensation of something so spiritual and so real. It's a feeling of freedom, like a bird soaring out of an open window. You have to come to terms with your sadness, your disappointments. You have to learn to forgive.

Think of it as a three-part process:

1. Write it Down: List out what you're holding onto. Write down the words "I forgive you" and feel them as you do.

3. Weigh the Pros and Cons: Make a list with two columns. In one column, write down the benefits of forgiving — peace, love, happiness, spirituality. In the other column, write down the costs of holding onto bitterness — anger, tears, sadness, feeling unloved. Ask yourself, "What if I continue to hold onto this? What if I let it go?"

4. Choose to Forgive: Look at your list. Which path leads to freedom? I can assure you that the decision to forgive will be the right one. Hate and misery only breed more hate and misery. Love, on the other hand, frees your mind, your soul, and the generations to come.

It's not easy, but you have to try — try very hard. Make your list, weigh your choices, and find the freedom that comes with forgiveness. I guarantee that, in the end, you will choose love, just like I did. I had to ask myself...

"What happens if I keep hating her?"

If I keep hating her, what does my life look like? It becomes filled with loneliness, disconnection, and bitterness.

If I choose to love her, then what? My life becomes filled with love, freedom, and peace.

WEIGHING THE PROS AND CONS

Think about something in your life that you are holding onto, something that has caused bitterness and pain and feels impossible to forgive. Take a moment to write down the pros of forgiving and creating freedom. Now, write down the cons of staying bitter and what you would continue to endure if you chose that path. What would your life look like if you chose to hold on to the anger? And what could your life look like if you chose to let it go?

A SCENARIO TO CONSIDER

Imagine this: You have a child, and your child's father abandoned both of you. As your child grows up, you try your best to explain the role of both Mom and Dad, despite the absence. One day, your child comes home and tells you, "I met my dad today." How do you respond?

Do you tell your child, "He's been gone for so long; you should hate him," or do you say, "He may have been absent for a while, but while he was gone, I was both your mom and dad. If you want to build a relationship with him, it's never too late. Choose to love, choose to forgive"?

What would you do? Would you pass on the pain from one generation to the next, or would you stop it here and now? The world is full of complexities, good and bad. No one is perfect. We all falter at some point. So, shouldn't we humble ourselves and choose forgiveness?

REFLECTING ON ANOTHER SITUATION

Think about it from another perspective: Suppose your spouse left you when your children were young. Then, one day, your daughter comes to you and says, "I want to meet my mom. I know she's living in this place." What would you do? Would you tell her, "Forget about your mom, hate her for the rest of your life, she's no good," or would you encourage her to forgive, to find love, and to seek peace?

What would you do? Would you choose to carry the burden of bitterness, or would you help guide the next generation toward love and forgiveness?

CHAPTER 17

BREAK FREE FROM
YOUR PAST

Creating a better future starts with living fully in the present. To do this, you must let go of the past. You must become an expert at letting go. Let go of anything that doesn't serve you—people, things, situations. Release anything that doesn't resonate with your frequency. Don't lower your frequency to match someone or something that's beneath where you're meant to be. Instead, seek out your tribe and stay in tune with your purpose, the one that aligns with where God wants you to be.

Think of it like tuning into a radio station. If you want to listen to FM 96.0, which broadcasts at that frequency, you can't tune into a lower station and expect to hear what's being broadcast on 96.0. This is how you should choose your community and the people you surround yourself with. Never lower your vibration to match someone else's if it means lowering yourself. Stay where you are meant to be.

LETTING GO IS RARELY EASY

Imagine this: you have a phone in your hand, an iPhone 15. You love it. You use it every day. It takes great pictures, has clear calls, and helps you stay connected. Then, a stranger approaches you with something hidden behind his back and asks you to give him your phone. Naturally, you say no—you know the value of your phone. He then asks, "What if I have something better for you?"

You don't know what he's hiding, so you hesitate. Why should you let go of something you know and value? But then you decide to take a leap of faith and let go of what's in your left hand—your iPhone. Immediately, he brings out a box from behind his back. Inside are not just one but several new gadgets: an iPhone 16, 17, 18, and 19, plus iPads and laptops—all of the highest quality and the fastest speed.

If you hadn't let go of your old phone, you wouldn't have had room to hold all these new blessings. Sometimes, you have to let go of what you're holding onto to receive something even greater.

But you trust and believe in the power of letting go.

Letting go can truly bring happiness, especially if the things you're holding onto no longer serve you. What if I had never let go of the anger and pain from my mom? I wouldn't be celebrating her today. I wouldn't be where I am today. I wouldn't be living in a state of love, peace, understanding, and being an ambassador of courage and service.

How can you serve others if you can't let go of what doesn't serve you? Love is unconditional. You have to let go of what doesn't serve you—

hate, bitterness, resentment. None of that serves you. Love does. I choose love over hate, any day.

Letting go isn't always easy, but it's necessary to create space for what is truly meant for you.

The most sought-after question and answer I sought as a child growing up was that of love and family; what is love and what is family. I never had the joy of such experiences growing up; just the pain, or maybe the negative effects of love I think, but over time I came to draw my very own conclusions, my own perspectives, based on how I was raised, what I was taught, from reading and experiencing humanity at all levels as I grew into a young man. I came to understand that love, though so simple, is the most complicated aspect of creation, humanity. I overwhelmingly came to the conclusion that believing in and loving your creator, your God, will lead to the true and purest understanding of love at the top most profound level you never anticipated.

Love is like the ocean, the depth, the width, the forces, the changing tides, the waves, every fish, every creature and all its inhabitants. It's impossible to truly love God without loving all that He has created, the majestic admirations of His perfect creations. Love is humanity, people, far and near, crossing every border, time zone, culture, languages, oceans, mountains, hills and valleys. Love extends far beyond to where the sun sets and rests; the divine light of the shining moon. Love is timeless and unconditional.

Understanding or grasping this idea, you are compelled to love what was / what's created by our Creator. How could we then shun our brothers and sisters, our children, family, our neighbors far and near.

The basis of life is love, love nourishes, cultivates, grows, embraces. I seek love because it is the essence of my being. To deny love to anyone is to deny our creator!

THE DIRT ROADS - JOIN MY JOURNEY

I remember as a young child walking up and down the dirt road that led from our house on the hill. We lived high up, and to get anywhere, we had to go down the hill to reach the flat roads. At that time, all the roads were dirt—no asphalt, just dirt. When it rained, whether a lot or a little, it would turn into a muddy mess. It was even worse being barefoot, with no shoes to protect my feet. Every step was filled with discomfort—rocks, sharp objects, even dog poop. My feet were always muddy.

When it rained, the mud would make walking treacherous. Sometimes, I would slip, and other times, the mud slowed me down, making every step feel like a struggle. The mud became an obstacle to my survival, to my ability to move forward and accomplish anything. The mud was my enemy, but perhaps not having shoes was my true enemy. Every rock felt like a knife digging into my feet. Sometimes, there were broken pieces of glass, and I could feel the sharpness cutting into my skin. In my country, we had things called prickles, and sometimes the rain would wash these prickles onto the path. Stepping on them would send waves of pain shooting through my feet.

Not having shoes was a constant discomfort, perhaps one of my greatest pains as a child.

DO THIS WHEN YOU'RE READY TO GIVE UP

I remember, as a child, having to carry water on my head in a bucket. The journey was over a mile and a half, at least two miles. I would walk down to the lowlands, fill the bucket, and make the long trek back up the hill to fill our water drum. We didn't have water lines where we lived, so we had to go down the hill—at least a mile and a half, maybe even closer to two miles—to get water.

This wasn't just a one-time trip. We would carry water all day long, starting in the morning and going up and down, up and down, up and down until the drums were full. I wasn't alone; my siblings were also carrying water, but it was still one of the most grueling tasks of my childhood. Carrying water on my head up and down that hill, over and over again, for a distance of approximately two miles was exhausting.

Thinking about it now, it seems almost insane—the idea of walking two miles down the hill and two miles back up, over and over again, just to have water. But this story is a reminder that, sometimes, you have to give everything you have for the thing that you need the most.

This is especially true when you have almost nothing left, and you're overwhelmed by everything you still have to do. Start with the ONE THING that matters most.

When you're in the hole, the thing you need most is a ladder of hope. Sure, you might have hundreds of other important things to think about. But everything depends on whether your ladder of hope is lowered down. If you're in a place where you're almost out of hope, motivation, and drive, take everything you have and invest it into what you need the most. This choice will strengthen your ability to focus all your attention on one thing, and that power will get you up off the ground when you feel like you don't have anything left. It will get you out of your hole. It will get you above ground. It will get you everything you want out of life.

www.ingramcontent.com/pod-product-compliance
Lightning Source LLC
Chambersburg PA
CBHW030311130626
46549CB00002B/810